I SWEAR I W

SEX PISTOLS AND THE SHAPE OF ROCK

ABOUT THE AUTHOR

David Nolan is a journalist and television producer. He has worked in newspapers, magazines, radio and television. He has also been a Government press adviser and a freelance writer for *Penthouse*. In 2000 he was awarded the Royal Television Society award for best current affairs programme for *Riot! – Strangeways Ten Years On*. He is married with two children.

He writes:
At the age of sixteen I started work on *Link-UP* magazine as a trainee reporter. Peter Oldham was a staff photographer at the time and was assigned to look after me.

He was 25 and had a blood-red, fuel-injection Ford Escort. Impossibly swish.

To pass the time travelling to interviews, we would talk about music. Peter claimed to have seen the Sex Pistols twice in 1976.

Bullshitter, I thought.

He then produced photographs he'd taken from the audience of Manchester's Free Trade Hall to prove it.

Bastard ...

At the time I told him there's a great documentary to be made about those gigs – the way they changed the face of music – maybe even a book.

Here it is.

David Nolan
Manchester 2001

I SWEAR I WAS THERE

SEX PISTOLS AND THE SHAPE OF ROCK

David Nolan

MILO BOOKS

First published 2001 by Milo Books in association with
Granada Media Commercial Ventures Limited

Copyright © Granada Media Group Limited 2001

David Nolan is the Author of this work

ISBN 1 903854 02 4

Typography and layout by
Derek Doyle and Associates, Liverpool

Printed and bound in Great Britain by
Guernsey Press Co Ltd, Guernsey

MILO BOOKS
P.O.Box 153
Bury
Lancs BL0 9FX
info@milobooks.com

Contents

To Katherine, Jake and Scott,
the only things more important to me than rock and roll.

Foreword

by Howard Devoto

A hundred or so punters turn up and Malcolm's quite pleased with me. Not too bad for 50p on a Friday evening. Inside, they like the Pistols all the way. The demand for an encore is insistent, even if they didn't get 'Woolly Bully' like some wag keeps shouting for.

'This is called "Problems". Where do you all come from?' Johnny Rotten is being friendly back.

Were some of the assembled on their feet by the start of the second encore? Can't remember. But there's a delay and Glen Matlock is saying into a mic something about the guitarist needing to change a guitar string. 'Who caaaaares???' someone yells. See? They've already got the idea.

Well, one of the ideas. *Ideas*.

Six weeks later. Tuesday. £1. Me and Pete Shelley have finally got our band together. I've scribbled the Buzzcocks set-list on the inside cover of one of my Castaneda books. Now it's come to it, I've realised I'm not up to stubbing cigarettes out on my body like Johnny reputedly does sometimes. And I had been planning to wash out a dog food tin, fill it with Fray Bentos pie filling, and eat it on stage with a fork to bait Slaughter and the Dogs. Hadn't got round to that either somehow.

Now the Pistols are due on. I stick my head round their dressing-room door.

'You ready?'

'Fuck off,' Johnny snarls at me.

Oh, right.

Howard Devoto – March 2001

Explanation

ONE OF THE many myths about the rock and roll band known as the Sex Pistols is that they did not play many gigs – either because they could not play, or because they were forever being banned by local councils.

Sex Pistols played 124 gigs before they imploded in an onstage, premeditated tizz at the Winterland Ballroom in San Francisco on January 14, 1978.

Not a bad strike rate.

Of those 124 gigs, the most important were the 27th and the 36th – because they inspired a new shape for rock. A new way to pick it up ... and a new way to run with it.

What came out of the two gigs at the Lesser Free Trade Hall in Manchester in 1976 has been a blueprint for the UK music scene that's lasted for twenty-five years.

Not punk-a-likes, sound-a-likes or spike-a-likes, not suburban boredom clones and public schoolboys faking angst, but new music.

Without gigs number 27 and 36 there would be no Buzzcocks, Magazine, Joy Division, New Order, Factory Records, no UK independent record system, no Fall, Smiths, Hacienda, Madchester, Happy Mondays, and Oasis. Without those two gigs, we would still be listening to everything and anything that 1976 had to offer. Despite them, maybe we still are ...

11

The point of this book – and the Granada Television documentary that shares the same name – is to sort out the many myths that have developed over the years about these two gigs ... and the Pistols' first ever television appearance, again at Granada TV.

Because of these myths, the other great thing about this period is the lovely, Mancunian cattiness that surrounds the whole story. I was there ... he wasn't ... she was there ... they DEFINITELY weren't.

One interviewee was asked if Mick Hucknall (Simply Red) was there: ' I didn't see no Charlie Drake lookalikes,' he replied.

The inaccuracies surrounding the whole thing are staggering (but to be expected): the lies that have been told are huge (ditto).

There are many people who have said *I Swear I Was There* for many years. Let's roll up our sleeves and sort the whole thing out.

1: Not Totally Loath to a Bit of Prog Rock

IN WHICH MR TRAFFORD AND MR MCNEISH TRY TO
GET THEIR 'SHIT' TOGETHER … AND FIND THAT
THEY ARE LACKING.

*IT IS A legendary piece of paper, although there are a number
of inaccuracies to be found on its time-yellowed face.*

The date printed on it is the Fourth of June 1076.

It claims to be 'plus Buzzcocks'.

It states that it will 'admit one'.

*Two out of three – as I believe Meatloaf once said – 'ain't
bad'.*

*On the admittance front, that much, at least, is correct.
The ticket did what it said – it admitted one . Although the
claims of the many, many people to have been one of those
admitted have to be taken with a pinch of salt.*

*That aside, it is a ticket for the Sex Pistols, live at the Lesser
Free Trade Hall, in Manchester, 4/6/76. To see Johnny Rotten,
Steve Jones, Glen Matlock and Paul Cook – young men
barely out of their teens – perform live on stage. The date
stamped on the ticket (1076) is 900 out of whack thanks
to some lazy hand-printing by the promoters. No matter.
In a way, the mistakes make it all the more special. This
particular ticket is kept in a brown envelope, along with*

The hand-typed ticket for the first Sex Pistols gig at the
Lesser Free Trade Hall, Manchester, with the year misprinted
(Courtesy: Peter Oldham)

some photographs, the negatives of which have been misplaced.

It is a noteworthy ticket for a concert twenty-five years ago. It is a ticket for the first of two gigs that changed the shape of rock.

The Buzzcocks never played at the first one. The band that really played is one of a hundred stories you're about to read, along with who was there, who wasn't there, and pictures and memories that have never been seen or heard before about those three events during the summer of 1976: the two gigs and that first-ever television appearance. Who told a handful of young, hirsute Mancunians to, 'Fuck off out of it'? Who threw peanuts at Slaughter and the Dogs? Who called Clive James a 'baldie old Sheila'? And who the hell are Gentlemen?

All in good time.

Sex Pistols did not come to Manchester: Manchester invited Sex Pistols to come to it. And for that we can thank two young men from different parts of Northern England who happened to come together in 1975. Peter McNeish and Howard Trafford were essentially responsible for everything that unfolds: two students who, after seeing the Pistols twice in February 1976, helped change the shape of rock. Two students who were soon to change their names to Pete Shelley and Howard Devoto.

HOWARD DEVOTO (Singer: Buzzcocks/Magazine): I spent my early childhood in the Midlands and then my teenage years in Leeds, so those were the years the hormones hit. *My early years?* My first ever love was The Shadows. After that I liked the Rolling Stones and after that I liked Bob Dylan, I liked Jimi Hendrix … things like The Mothers of Invention, and then David Bowie. I went to college, Bolton Institute of Technology, in 1972, messed around trying to do a Psychology degree for a year and a half, packed that up, went back and did a Humanities degree. This brings us up to the more pertinent years.

What I always remember of my time then really is buying *Fun House* (1970) by The Stooges. I didn't really know any Stooges fans, and their records were very hard to get hold of although *Raw Power* had come out in '73 and I did manage to get a copy at the local record shop in Bolton. That was about it. Then I managed to pick up a secondhand copy of their first album (*The Stooges*, 1969) from somewhere or other. But *Fun House* was proving quite hard to track down. I wasn't quite sure I liked The Stooges that much. I liked the story, I liked the legend, but for me, *Raw Power* was a bit messy, the first Stooges album was a little simplistic. But then when I finally managed to get an import copy of *Fun House* it all fell into place. It just kind of hit me at the time when I was starting to get really pissed off again in life. I have this memory of myself at this place I was living – 'The Convent' as we all called it, since it was an ex-Convent that had been taken over for student accommodation – in my room there playing *Fun House* and just loving the primitive nature of it and the anger of it. I just really connected with it and started to think 'I could just about do this'.

15

TONY WILSON (TV presenter/head of Factory Records): It's hard to describe how bloody awful music was, how desperately bad it was, how our Sixties heroes had become boring and useless and how the stuff that was happening then, not only was it bad ... they were badly dressed. The only music I was listening to in late '75 was Austin, Texas country music. The rest of it was a wasteland of boredom and *The Old Grey Whistle Test*.

Between Christmas and New Year (1975/6) a kid called Dennis Brown who was a deadhead from university, a mate of mine, gave me the Patti Smith *Horses* album. God, it was fantastic and different and wonderful

PETE SHELLEY (Buzzcocks): Yes (progressive rock band) albums were getting longer and longer than most people's recorded output.

MARK E. SMITH (lead singer: The Fall): I was working on the docks at the time. I wasn't long out of school. The stuff I used to like was mid-Sixties American trash bands ... garage stuff like The Seeds, The Stooges, things like that. A bit of trashy soul, dub reggae. I didn't like anything that was out at the time. You just weren't interested really – a bit like now. Radio was a no-no. At the time, I thought the best Manchester band was probably The Hollies or Freddie and the Dreamers. We were doing poetry to guitars, but we were doing it in our flat. Someone would read a poem out – we had a bass player who was into Jaco Pastorious – that was very much influenced by Patti Smith. You didn't think of actually attempting to play live. You had to have a drummer and lights, all that sort of thing.

PAUL MORLEY (audience member/journalist): Stockport Technical College had two or three gigs a year.

'I had no knowledge of The Ramones, of the New York Dolls, I wasn't even aware of Iggy': TV presenter Tony Wilson in 1976

Elton John came when I was thirteen which just seemed like manna from heaven. It was just the most extraordinary thing. They wouldn't have groups play there, but they would often have film of groups playing. I remember they had a film of Jimi Hendrix, which was the biggest thing that happened in 1975.

JORDAN (shop assistant/punk muse): I come from a place near Brighton – and Brighton was really quite a hip place – a lot of great clubs there, usually gay clubs. There's still bands that I really love – Iggy Pop, Lou Reed, David Bowie – I guess quite a lot of people say that that was what they were listening to early on, before the Pistols, before punk. I think people see that as the grounding really for punk.

IAN MOSS (audience member): You can never just say everything was a load of rubbish. But there was a lot of rubbish out there ... really hideous, a lot of it. And disgusting. And pompous. And American.

MICK ROSSI (Slaughter and the Dogs): Any good band, they're going to have *Ziggy Stardust*, they're going to have *Transformer*, they're going to have *Slaughter on Tenth Avenue*, they're going to have Marc Bolan records there. It's just a great grounding for anyone those records.

The punk rock musical touchstones tend to be a shared experience, at least publicly. The same names occur: The Stooges, The MC5, The New York Dolls, Roxy Music, David Bowie and bands that made it onto Elektra Records' Nuggets compilation album in 1972 such as The Standells and ? & The Mysterians. But what about more primitive UK influences like the bare-bones R 'n' B of Dr Feelgood, formed in 1971, and Eddie and the Hot Rods, who came together four years later? Perhaps they are often ignored because they came bearing the unfashionable beer-brown stain of what was, by this time in 1976, last month's thing – pub rock.

WILL BIRCH (musician/author: *No Sleep Till Canvey Island – The Great Pub Rock Revolution*): Dr Feelgood and Eddie and the Hot Rods did have influence over the punk rock groups. The speed at which they took the music and their onstage aggression was inherited. The Feelgoods and the Hot Rods primed the audience for the Sex Pistols and the Clash. There was a young audience, mainly eighteen-year-old blokes who had seen the Feelgoods, seen the Hot Rods and bought *Stupidity* (Dr Feelgood's third album, 1976) and *Teenage Depression* (Eddie and the Hot Rods 1976). When the Sex Pistols came along it was, 'Hey, yeah, we're ready for this.' I'm not so sure so many people would have been ready to embrace the Sex Pistols had it not have been for that ground work.

PAUL MORLEY: I'd been interested in pop music and I'd fallen in love with Mark Bolan when I was young, but I was also interested in all sorts of stranger kinds of music, things like the Velvet Underground and The Stooges and I was into strange German alternative music, free jazz. Patti Smith had just happened and that front cover of *Horses* with a black and white shot that Mapplethorpe did with the skinny tie and the white shirt ... it seemed so full of colour and life even though it was monochrome. Dr Feelgood seemed incredibly relevant, because the songs were short and sharp and fast and ferocious and angry ... and seemed to be cutting away all the fat and flab and artificiality that there was elsewhere in the more commercial record company types of music. And The Ramones had just happened from New York.

GLEN MATLOCK (bass guitar: Sex Pistols): The Glam Rock thing was over. There had been a pub rock thing which hadn't really made it. Bands like Yes and Barclay James Harvest didn't really touch the kids in the street around my way. Punk was something that kids could identify with and get their teeth into. Everybody was looking for something at the same time. It was there because we was just that little bit ahead of the game. We were like the standard bearers for the movement and everybody rallied around us. When we came up to Manchester and started playing around a bit, we had a little bit of press by then. We'd already got an inkling

19

of, you know, here's something new. So they came, dare I say it, with a bit more of an open mind about it, than maybe we'd had when we'd been doing some little club in London.

HOWARD DEVOTO: I also was not totally loath to a little bit of prog rock. I do remember going along to the college gigs every Saturday night, but really getting very fed up with it and feeling, I wish I could go and see The Stooges or something like that, something that's really going to be confrontational and aggressive and exciting and a bit dangerous

EDDIE GARRITY (Ed Banger and The Nosebleeds): Well I was a big Slade fan at the time so I was following them by the time they came along. Anything with Roxy, anything like that or Bowie ... more the harder edge sort of bands.

TONY WILSON: (At that time) you've got John Miles, the guitarist, you get Be-Bop Deluxe, you get Eddie and the Hot Rods, who were kind of a pop pre-cursor.

PAUL MORLEY: At the beginning of '76, I was eighteen and turned nineteen just before the Sex Pistols came up. I know it sounds crazy now but at the time we were still coming out of the war, it was still a bleak kind of time and we'd just come out of the three day week and life was a lot more minimal and sparse. Sparser than it is now, when it's so full of stimulation and signs of pop culture. Back then it was very raw and naked. And so even though I was eighteen, nineteen, it could have been fourteen, fifteen today. You were still kind of trying to find a way to rebel, there wasn't processed rebellion, the rebellion wasn't packaged like it is now and marketed to segments of teen life. It was something you discovered for yourself. Looking back, I think of myself as being very young, I'm surprised how kind of naïve I was in a way. But I was definitely trying to find something out for myself that would help me, rather than what I was being told was the way forward.

HOWARD DEVOTO: I started the second year of my course. I'd had a slightly unfortunate encounter with exams – I didn't do that brilliantly in my first year – so when I went into the second year of my course I was kind of looking round for other things to get involved with and one of the things I did was to stick up a notice at college, asking to meet musicians. I mentioned the name of The Stooges in the advert and 'Sister Ray' (Velvet Underground) and stuff like this. Possibly, Pete (Shelley) was the only person who answered that advert. No, he wasn't the only person but he was the only person I kind of stuck with. We'd been trying things with a drummer ... some Stooges songs, trying some (Brian) Eno songs, even trying some early Rolling Stones songs. But it really was not happening. So by February 1976, I don't think we really knew where any of this was going except that we were vaguely still trying to get a band together.

Peter McNeish (Shelley) was from Leigh in what is now called Greater Manchester. Although he was three years younger than Howard Devoto, McNeish was way ahead of him in terms of organisation. He had already been involved with bands at Leigh Grammar School. The bands were called Kogg and then Jets of Air. He learned how to hire halls, how to play gigs and he actually made money. These were entrepreneurial skills that were about to be put to very good use.

PETE SHELLEY: We're to blame for lots of things! We were quite strange, Jets of Air. As well as my own songs, we used to do Roxy Music, Velvet Underground and David Bowie covers. It was hard to get gigs really. There was always the pub rock circuit but you had to play songs that people knew, basically do like a 'living juke box'. Most of the gigs we did were ones which we organised ourselves, so I'd go and hire a local hall and sell tickets. The money used to balance out. If you overestimate the cost and underestimate the profit and if you could still make it break even, then you're on a sure-fire winner. So it was just a case of trying to find places to play. We even played a Christian society meeting at a party at Bolton Grammar school, which was strange.

HOWARD DEVOTO: Pete claims that the Jets of Air came from some kind of phrase he got in a chemistry or physics lesson. I believe him.

No actual Trafford-McNeish band existed at this stage, but lots of album-listening did.

HOWARD DEVOTO: John Cale (Velvet Underground), his solo albums. *Fear* (1974) was a really important record to me. Then I did discover the Velvet Underground very late. Eno songs were among the earliest we would sort of practice with. We'd even try to perform. So there was a sort of contingent of people that seemed to be kind of interesting before the Patti Smiths. One was reading about all that happening in New York but you couldn't hear any of it.

As well as record devotion, there was avid reading of the music press. One article in particular caught the eye of

Trafford and McNeish. The article would take them across the country. It changed their names and it changed their lives.

HOWARD DEVOTO: *New Musical Express* came out in Bolton and I kind of flipped through it, gave it to Pete. He looked through it and handed it back to me and said, 'Did you read that?' and this was the first ever review of the Sex Pistols by Neil Spencer (*New Musical Express*, February 21, 1976) ... 'DON'T LOOK OVER YOUR SHOULDER BUT THE SEX PISTOLS ARE COMING'. The Stooges were mentioned in there and 'We're not into music, we're into chaos'. There was that line in there. Well it clicked with me and it just so happened I could borrow a car that weekend. I didn't have a car, but somebody in the house I was living in at that time, had asked me to pick up their car and said, 'You can borrow it for the weekend.' I don't think they meant 'you can drive to London for the weekend' but anyway that's what Pete and I ended up doing. Just on the basis of reading this review and the fact that I could borrow this car. It was the weekend that changed our lives.

MALCOLM MCLAREN (manager: Sex Pistols): Howard was a guy, I think, that picked up on a small article in the *NME* about the Sex Pistols ... and how dreadful they were.

McLaren was a shopkeeper. The store he ran with Vivienne Westwood at 430 King's Road, Chelsea, had previously been a supplier of New Edwardian (Teddy Boy) gear called Let It Rock, later re-named Too Fast to Live, Too Young to Die. By the time Shelley and Devoto arrived, it was billed as being run by 'specialists in rubberwear, glamourwear and stagewear' and went by the name of Sex. The band that virtually shared the shop's name was there to sell the couture – or 'trousers' if you prefer ... the Sex Pistols. Front of house at Sex was the living embodiment of the shop's ethos, Pauline Rook – the shop assistant also known as Jordan.

JORDAN: I decided that after I'd done my A levels, I wanted to come up to London with a purpose to work for Vivienne (Westwood) and Malcolm (McLaren) in their shop in King's Road (Too Fast to Live, Too Young to Die/ Sex). I got an interim job with Harrods with the hope that maybe I'd get a job at Vivienne's. I walked in one day and had quite a long talk with the manager, and I guess he liked the way I looked and Malcolm liked the way I looked. A few days later I got called up and asked if I'd do an afternoon. That afternoon lasted for some years. Boy George used to come in the shop, he used to come to lots of gigs and buy a lot of clothes from Vivienne, he always seemed to have a lot of money ... (*laughing*) ... I'll have to ask him one day where he got it from.

HOWARD DEVOTO: We first met Malcolm when we turned up at Sex, his shop, having been told by Neil Spencer at the *New Musical Express* – who I'd phoned – that, 'Oh I think their manager runs the Sex shop on King's Road.' So we were vaguely expecting to turn up to an Ann Summers-type shop.

JORDAN: I'd been, I suppose for want of a better description, the front person of Vivienne's shop. A lot of glossy girl magazines used to come and take photos and talk to me about what the shop was all about. I was dressing very crazy at that time, very Fifties ... bouffant, black eyeliner, sort of 'Cleopatra goes Fifites' ... with lots of ripped tights and stilettos and Perspex clothes. I was doing my own thing, buying my own clothes, down in Sussex, which was really comparable with what Malcolm and Vivienne were doing up in London.

I commuted for about two years. I had some really bad do's on the train – I had tourists trying to pay me for my photo ... worse than that, mothers saying that I'm upsetting their children and debauching them and how dare I get on a train looking like that. Somebody tried to throw me off the train one day, literally out the door. So British Rail told me to go and sit in first class, get out of trouble. Me sitting on the train in my rubber gear and what have you, a few men used to get a bit het up as well. I think that might have caused a bit of a stir.

PETE SHELLEY: They said, 'There's this guy who's got this shop on the King's Road.' So we started off at Sloane Square and walked all the way down. Got there and they were just closing up. So we asked him and he said, 'Oh yeah, the boys are playing in High Wycombe.' We saw two shows that weekend and it was great. Howard was talking to Malcolm and Malcolm was saying that he wanted to have a gig outside of London 'cause all he could get was little gigs.

HOWARD DEVOTO: I remember Jordan was there, and Malcolm turned up a short while later, in his black leather stuff ... well, they're desperately cool, aren't they? So I don't expect anybody was going, 'Oh wow ... you've come all the way down from Manchester to see us.' Malcolm turned up and of course at that point we didn't even know whether they were playing, we'd come down totally on spec. We bought our copy of *Time Out*, where we got the name Buzzcocks from (a story about TV music show *Rock Follies* carries the headline 'IT'S THE BUZZ, COCK!') Can't find anything about them. When we finally meet Malcolm we learn, oh yes, they are actually playing tonight and supporting Malcolm and Vivienne's mate Screaming Lord Sutch.

JORDAN: When The Pistols came along, it seemed to come together really quickly. I used to go to rehearsals sometimes, I mean that was pretty dodgy. I never had any doubt whatsoever. That old adage about the clothes and the music coming together – it was one of the first times in history where a look was actually created for a band that people could buy. I just knew they were going to do it, if they hadn't had those clothes they would have still done it. If they hadn't had the Malcolm and the Vivienne ethic behind them, I think they would have still done it.

TONY WILSON: Malcolm wanted, in the Pistols, to create the Bay City Rollers of outrage. He wanted a band who couldn't play, who swore, who were just appalling ... and who would be number one just cause they were disgusting. In fact, they became number one because they were fantastic. Culturally ... musically, even. Malcolm, I always think he got screwed by art. He actually created a great artwork and he didn't really want that. He wanted to create something that was actually valueless and would make some kind of political joke. Instead, he got this great moment in cultural history.

JORDAN: Malcolm had a huge influence on them, but there's no way you could make somebody do those things. They had a positive attitude and it just seemed to bring the youth of the whole country together. Working in a shop in King's Road you would have people coming from absolutely everywhere to buy stuff there. It was a real treat, it was a pilgrimage down to King's Road.

HOWARD DEVOTO: Everything about the Sex Pistols impressed at that first gig we went to at High Wycombe (College of Higher Education 20/2/76) and the second one. They repeated the experience the following evening at Welwyn Garden City (21/2/76). Most importantly, the music, and for me, the lyrics. We could hear some interesting lyrics going on in there. The aggro of it was interesting. At that first gig, John (Johnny Rotten) got into a bit of a tussle with somebody in the audience and kept singing under a small pile of people. That was sort of what one had been looking for for quite a while. He would get his hanky out and stick it up his nose and he'd wander off the stage for five minutes and then come back. Just right spot on. Impressed. I mean, at that time his look was a kind of skinhead look – but a different take on that. The ripped sweater – it was just different. Pete and I immediately had a model. When we saw the Pistols, we'd got a musical model.

PETE SHELLEY: They enjoyed the same kind of music that me and Howard liked. I mean they were playing 'No Fun' and we liked The Stooges. They were playing short sharp songs, even their version of 'Stepping Stone' (most famously recorded by The Monkees) was a wonder to behold. We saw them doing it and we thought, well, if they can do it we can do it. Howard and I decided that we would make it, happen rather than just writing songs and not do anything. So we worked towards making our dream a reality.

HOWARD DEVOTO: I went up to Malcolm after they'd played and said, 'If we could organise for you to play at our college, are you interested in coming up to do it?' And he said, 'Yeah, sure, if you can arrange it, we'll come up and do it.'

I think the Pistols were kind of chuffed: 'Wow, these guys have come all the way down from Manchester to see us.'

PETE SHELLEY: I mean, we were up North! They were wearing Vivienne Westwood clothes. We just made our own. All the gigs they could get were basically within the M25, if it existed then – I don't know – but all it had been up to then was just Greater London. It was the only place they could get gigs, so the idea was that if we get something outside of London then at least it's onward and upwards ...

Howard Devoto and Pete Shelley – as they have now named themselves – returned home in their borrowed car, determined to bring the Sex Pistols north. The first problem was where to play. The obvious choice was their own college. The Pistols' Manchester debut should have actually been at the Bolton Institute of Technology, but the college's powers-that-be talked themselves out of a place in rock history.

HOWARD DEVOTO: When Pete and I got back to college, despite Pete's clout in the Students Union, they weren't going for it – not interested in putting them on. Malcolm might have said something like, you know, 'We don't want to play a pub', because of course pub rock was kind of the vibe that consciously or unconsciously people were trying to get away from. It might have been hippies and prog rock at a higher level, but at a lower level it was pub rock.

WILL BIRCH: When a lot of the punk rock groups came out they claimed to be influenced by the New York Dolls,

The Stooges and The MC5. But none of those American groups sold very many records in the UK. So I think there was a little bit of bandwagon jumping in that respect. They did owe quite a lot to the preceding pub rock era. What pub rock did, immediately before punk rock, was to establish a network of venues and infrastructure.

The venue that Shelley and Devoto ended up hiring out was definitely not a pub. The Free Trade Hall was one of Manchester's biggest venues, and played host to the big bands of the day. Above it was a mini version, an all-seated auditorium called the Lesser Free Trade Hall.

PETE SHELLEY: We found out we could hire the Lesser Free Trade Hall for about £32 or something. And just doing the maths we knew that if we got forty people in we would be in profit. So it seemed like a good idea.

HOWARD DEVOTO: So when I phoned Malcolm and told him, 'They're not going for it,' he said, 'Well, see if you can find somewhere else ... we'll come up and play.' We somehow learned about this little hall above the Free Trade Hall, called the Lesser Free Trade Hall ... as if it's some kind of curious bird, you know, 'a lesser-spotted auditorium' ... It was not a lot of money, so I got back to Malcolm again. 'Yeah, okay hire it!' So I made sure he sent me a cheque to cover the payment. So, that first gig for June 4, 1976, was suddenly on the cards. He (McLaren) paid for the hall so it wasn't going to be a huge disaster if nobody turned up. The main thing that would have been bugging me and Pete was the fact that our bloody group wasn't ready.

PETE SHELLEY: We didn't have a bass player or a drummer and so that was our sticking point.

Despite having booked the Lesser Free Trade Hall – and the Sex Pistols – it became increasingly apparent that Devoto and Shelley's band would not be able, to use the parlance of the day, to get their 'shit' together in time to support their London heroes.

HOWARD DEVOTO: We didn't know a load of musicians, we weren't on any musician circuit. It was just very, very difficult to find people. Just the usual problems you have when you've got no money ... nowhere to rehearse. We just couldn't make it happen. I'm still at college, trying to be a promoter for the first time. Just arranging it for the Sex Pistols – in itself that was a really big thrill at that point in my life.

PETE SHELLEY: We were sticking up posters so that maybe more people would find out about the gig. But also the Sex Pistols were getting write ups in music papers on a regular basis and so it seemed more and more people had heard that something was happening ... and they started checking it out.

Devoto and Shelley resigned themselves to the roles of promoters/organisers/ticket printers. The Free Trade Hall had been host to many legendary concerts, but not many people knew of its little cousin up above.

PETE SHELLEY: The Lesser Free Trade Hall is up the stairs. It's usually used for like lectures before classical concerts: 'Go in, find out what Beethoven really meant.' It was just available for hire. It held about three hundred people.

Pete Shelley may believe it was 'just available for hire', but others can throw harsher light on the history of the building.

PHIL GRIFFIN (writer on architecture): It's on the site of the Peterloo Massacre (a political reform rally that ended with a charge by the military: eleven people died, literally, by the sword). It is, after all, the only civic building that I know that's named after a radical political movement ... the Free Trade Movement, the Anti-Corn Law League.

Italianate is what people tend to call it. Architect? David Walters, 1853. A high Victorian respect for Italian buildings is what it demonstrates. As with a lot of buildings at the time, it's all front. It's always been a place where young people and audiences have gathered in order to express themselves in one way or another. Until very recently it has been a place for trade union meetings. There's many a strike been voted in the Free Trade Hall. There's certainly been a history of radicalism in terms of its performance. I'm referring to the famous 1965 concert when a member of the audience at the Manchester Free Trade Hall – not the Albert Hall as many believe – accused Bob Dylan of being 'Judas'. Strong words, in my view. I was there that night and gradually the Free Trade Hall emptied. The first set was acoustic and familiar, then on marched these people who clearly the audience hadn't invited, making noises they weren't familiar with. They got most upset about it. People even write books about it.

MARK E. SMITH: The Free Trade Hall was ... not sacred ... it was like *so* crap. Been to a few shows there, most of the bands that are coming back now – it's like a time warp for me.

PAUL MORLEY: The Manchester Free Trade Hall was like this cathedral of conventional, established sounds. You'd see your Pink Floyds and your David Bowies and your T-Rex's and so that was incredibly exciting. But they played the Lesser Free Trade Hall ... this sort of part of the Free Trade that you didn't know anything about. In fact, the only time I'd come across the Lesser Free Trade Hall before is when some theatre company had done a performance of *Waiting for Godot*, where they all acted it out as members of the IRA. So, the idea that the Sex Pistols were playing there, that was also incredibly kind of unusual. It was a very shrewd choice by Howard Devoto to put them there, because it could have just been a grungy little dirty club or somewhere difficult to get to. Because it was the Lesser Free Trade Hall, you kind of knew how to get to it. I know that sounds strange but for a long time, I thought underground music was something that genuinely happened underground, that you couldn't go unless you looked a certain way, smelt a certain way and dressed a certain way. So the fact that it was at the Lesser Free Trade Hall, that made it very accessible ... Oh, I can get to that, I know how to get tickets for the Lesser Free Trade Hall ... you just go to the box office. So the whole thing had this kind of fantastic mystery and distance, but also seemed very close.

By late May 1976, Howard Devoto and Pete Shelley were doing everything in their power to make sure as many people as possible managed to find their way to the Lesser Free Trade.

HOWARD DEVOTO: McLaren certainly sent up some A3 posters that he'd got printed off. Malcolm was quite good with Jamie Reid (Situationist partner-in-crime of McLaren and instigator of the 'blackmail' style of lettering common to a lot of Pistols/punk artwork) because of his background in putting together press packs, which did have a fairly strong design element. The thing that impressed us about them (the press packs) was that they put in all the bad reviews as well. Pete (Shelley) and I were suddenly in the fly-post business. We did go up and down Oxford Road (major road into Manchester city centre) pasting these A3 things which, at the end of the day, were trying to double as leaflets and posters. They weren't very imposing and whether they managed to pull in anybody, I've no idea. At the end of May, probably barely a week before the first gig, a cassette tape turned up (with Pistols demos). We thought, they sound great. I copied the cassette onto my reel-to-reel, because I wasn't advanced enough to have a cassette player. I can't remember quite what my contact with Tony Wilson was but I got this tape to him.

Tony Wilson was a Salford-born Cambridge graduate who was several years into his career in television. After working as a trainee at ITN, he returned North to Granada Television, where he was a reporter and presenter for Granada Reports, the tea-time news magazine programme that served the North West of England, an area of the country known at the time as Granadaland. As a presenter on news and the So It Goes programme, Wilson had developed a sarky style that seemed designed to wind audiences up. At home, my parents always referred to him as 'That Tony Wilson'. Wilson knew something was up when he started to get strange things in the mail, which he received at his desk at Granada Television's studios on Quay Street in Manchester.

TONY WILSON: Manchester was the fertile breeding ground, the field ready ploughed, ready tilled, just ready to receive these seeds. It was the perfect punk city. The history of rock and roll was the history of small cities. I sat around in those first six months waiting to do this 'comedy show', bored shitless by the bands. Then two things happened to me. One, I got one of those Wilton packaging, brown cardboard LP sleeves. Inside it was this battered copy of the New York Dolls album cover. No vinyl with it. I presume Mozzer kept his vinyl at home. The note was from this Stretford schoolboy called Steven Morrisey (later lead singer of The Smiths) saying, 'Why can't there be more bands like this?' Then I got this cassette through the post, saying 'Dear Mr Wilson ...' It was from someone called Howard Trafford. He said there's a new band from London, they're coming to Manchester on June 4, I think you'll like them. I've still got the cassette box, but someone nicked the cassette. I think one of the tracks was 'Pretty Vacant'.

HOWARD DEVOTO: I had no idea who Tony Wilson was. Somehow or other I got in touch with Tony and I got this tape to him. That's the degree of contact really that I remember. It's the same degree that I remember with Malcolm. I did meet up with him briefly when I went down to see Bowie play at the Empire Pool, now Wembley Stadium. Malcolm looked down his nose at that; Bowie was not to be conjured with in his books. The main thing that was going on at that time in the music press was that mentions of them (Sex Pistols) were getting more and more frequent. I'm not quite sure at what point they made the front page in *Melody Maker*, but their profile was building in the music papers

TONY WILSON: In May (1976) I'd gone to the Roundhouse in London. We couldn't get a permit to film Patti Smith but I was able to at least interview her. She was having PMT at the time so it was a bloody nightmare. She was appalling.

Hanging around waiting for her all afternoon in the Roundhouse, I sat in some side room with this young *NME* journalist. It was (Tony) Parsons. We sat there, swinging our legs at this table and he was telling me about this band I was going to see in two weeks time – the Pistols. He thought they were fantastic. So yes, there's this swell all the way throughout that first six months of '76, there' s this swell of maybe something happening. It's hard to remember now that we're used to the continuous re-birth in pop music, that however bad it gets ... it will get exciting again. That first time, it might never have got exciting again, it might never have changed.

Which is why, sitting in that old theatre seat on June 4 and watching this Pistols thing was such a shock. I'm very lucky, I was at the first one. Because the first one was utterly and painfully outrageous and wonderful ... I'm Gig One.

Buzzcocks did manage a gig of sorts, two months before the Pistols' Manchester gig. They played songs by David Bowie and the Rolling Stones. Badly.

PETE SHELLEY: A complete disaster. I think there were three songs. The first song lasted about twenty minutes ... even though it wasn't supposed to. There were things borrowed and stolen but part of it was just getting back to short songs and the more direct delivery ... just making music exciting again.

HOWARD DEVOTO: The debut of an entity called Buzzcocks actually took place on April 1 at Bolton Institute of Technology. I was there in my new drainpipes and knee-length pink boots, feeling very splendid.

PETE SHELLEY: Howard went to a boutique and chose a pair of trousers and said he wanted them altering. He said, I want them taking in cause everything was flares, so he had them taken in so they were almost drainpipes .. and the guy said, 'Are you sure about this? Because after it's done, they won't be able to stitch it back together. You've ruined the trousers.' He (Howard) could stop traffic by walking in tight trousers, it was amazing.

HOWARD DEVOTO: I think we might have played 'Oh Shit!' ... 'No Reply' ... 'Get On Our Own' ... things like that. We hadn't written any co-compositions like 'Breakdown' ... 'Times Up' ... certainly not 'Boredom'. We got the plug pulled on us after three numbers.

PETE SHELLEY: It meant that instead of thinking about doing it, we'd actually done it. Because if you think about doing things, there's always problems and you're trying to think of ways of solving that problem, even though the problem may never arise, so by doing things ... you actually get them done, not by thinking about it. You have to think about them to a certain extent but at some point you have to trust the fact that you are going to do it, or not ... it's a bit like riding a bike ... take off your jockey wheels and give yourself a big push and hope for the best.

Despite minor setbacks to the career of the Buzzcocks, the idea of the Sex Pistols – and indeed punk rock – was spreading swiftly across Manchester. It was also making inroads, perhaps more importantly, into the suburbs. And it was the young residents of these suburbs that found their way to the Lesser Free Trade Hall on June 4, 1976.

2: Intimidation on Legs

IN WHICH THE SEX PISTOLS ARE BROUGHT TO MANCHESTER
TO PLAY A CONCERT – FEATURING CONFUSION OVER
ATTENDANCE AND SUPPORT PLAYERS.

*THE SUBURBAN youths who took the trouble to make their
way to the Lesser Free Trade Hall on 4 June 1976 were about
to see the Sex Pistols in their 'punk' prime. That is 'punk' in
the old-fashioned sense of the word. Trashy, garage band,
Sixties-obsessed and power-chorded. Rock music un-
glammed yet deprived of denim. The name and reputation
of the band reached far across what is now known as
Greater Manchester.*

PETER HOOK (Joy Division/NewOrder/Monaco): I
was living in Little Hulton (near Bolton). I used to read
the newspapers quite avidly so I was interested in it, but
I just didn't realise what was happening. I remember
getting the *Melody Maker* and on the front cover there was
a picture of a group fighting at a gig ... and it was the Sex
Pistols. I thought, my God, this is not the normal thing! I
used to read the *Manchester Evening News* cover to cover
all the time and I spotted a little tiny advert for the Lesser
Free Trade Hall for the Sex Pistols plus support. It was
50p.

Glen Matlock and Johnny Rotten onstage at the Lesser Free Trade Hall
on June 4, 1976

IAN MOSS (audience member): There had been a piece
in the *New Musical Express* about a gig they played and
there was a photograph of the fracas. There was a quote –
the famous quote, 'It's not about the music, it's the chaos' or
something. That interested you, because prior to that, it
was all about horrible musiciany things that normal people
didn't know about, like scales and beats to a bar.

PAUL MORLEY (audience member/journalist): I
worked in a bookshop in Stockport. I left school and didn't
know what I wanted to do. I worked in this bookshop and it
was kind of like my university in a way, it was an education.
I'll always remember that nobody would come in the shop
on a Wednesday, so I would just read and read and read. I
was really into music and I used to nip into Manchester

where I found a shop that sold bootlegs – Dylan and Led Zeppelin bootlegs.

PETER OLDHAM (audience member/photographer):
I grew up in Denton (Tameside, Greater Manchester). I went to Art College doing a photographic course ... but always with an interest in music. Come Thursday, get the *NME*, scour through it, see what was on, go and see bands. We always thought the performance was a lot more valuable than a record. So to go into town (Manchester) and go down to the Free Trade Hall was nice, cheap entertainment. The kind of bands? Camel, Uriah Heep, all the old concept bands ... all very stodgy really but it was good fun. It was basically all that was on offer ... what was about at the time. Then punk came along ... that night, as it happens.

PAUL MORLEY: As soon as certain writers you really favoured started writing in an interesting way about the Sex Pistols, plus their name, plus their look, plus the names of the people in the group ... as soon as you heard there was any chance of them coming up to Manchester, you had to be interested in that.

ALAN HEMPSHALL (audience member/musician):
Levenshulme, Manchester ... born and bred there. Born in September 1960. I was still living at home at the time in question, June 4, 1976. I was fifteen years old. I think Levenshulme had an ambience of being slightly better off than North Manchester, it wasn't pure Coronation Street, there were little gardens in the front.
Obviously *Sounds* and *NME* were a must. I used to buy *Sounds* strangely more than *NME*, but obviously it varied depending on who was on the front cover. I went to school

41

in Gorton, and you had a choice of the Glam Rock and everybody was into Bowie or Alice Cooper. If you wanted to get a bit more cerebral then you got into Led Zeppelin or you got into Emerson, Lake and Palmer.

TONY WILSON: Was Alan at it? Fucking hell!

Meanwhile, the Pistols were heading North, expecting to get full support from the promised Devoto/Shelley band. Despite the gig in Bolton on April 1, they felt, quite rightly, that they just weren't ready. So despite the fact that the tickets had already been made and quite clearly stated that the gig would feature the Sex Pistols + Buzzcocks, a replacement band had to be found. There was no way they could charge 50p to see just one band, even if that band was the Sex Pistols.

HOWARD DEVOTO: Because we weren't ready, we needed to draft somebody else in to play support (for the Pistols). We didn't know anybody. The only thing I could remember was this guy – I think his name was Geoff – that I worked with the previous summer at a mail-order warehouse in Manchester doing a holiday job as a student, this guy there that was in a band.

So, despite what the posters said ... despite what the tickets said ... the Sex Pistols were not supported by the Buzzcocks on June 4, 1976. They were supported by Howard's workmate/pretend friend. There's been a lot of confusion surrounding this over the years – and If any writers have gone this far previously, the following mistake usually occurs.

PETE SHELLEY: There was a band called the Mandela Band or Mandala Band. Don't know which one it was. They were a bit 'hippy trippy' type thing. I never saw them because I was collecting the tickets.

HOWARD DEVOTO: It was a group called Solstice, not the Mandala Band. They did things like 'Nantucket Sleighride' which is, I think, a tune by Mountain. I just remember Geoff in this white boiler suit.

PETE SHELLEY: It could have been Solstice. It could have been. I think Howard would probably know because he conspired with them ... but we never played with them again after that.

TONY WILSON: Why did I go? Maybe there was this feeling, there was an appetite ... Oh my God, there's something new. I mean now, I walk around the world, desperate and waiting and I go and see anything, because it might be the new thing. Good God ... I'd even go to Leeds. Why did I go? Anyway I go ... it was in the diary, June the fourth.

HOWARD DEVOTO: On the night of the first gig, I was probably running around the hall, doing all the kinds of things you do ... trying to make sure it all happens. I'd just bought the first Ramones album on import – and I discovered the house PA system – so, I was doing the interval music.

TONY WILSON: I had no knowledge of The Ramones. I had no backwards knowledge, as the Stretford schoolboy Morrisey had, of the New York Dolls. And I wasn't even really aware of Iggy.

PETE SHELLEY: I was in a box office selling tickets and

Malcolm was coming down to see how many people were wandering around outside the chalk board ... big letters, 'LIVE FROM LONDON – THE SEX PISTOLS', (saying things to people like) 'Oh there's this band from London ... the Sex Pistols, they're great, they're fantastic, they're really famous.' So it was all a big game. It was all a big con trick to get people to part with £1.

One of those who fell for this was Steve Diggle, later of the Buzzcocks. Diggle would never have ended up in the band if he hadn't fallen for Malcolm's spiel.

PETE SHELLEY: We didn't have a bass player or a drummer. Howard had a phone call that afternoon on June 4 from somebody who left a message, saying they were a bass player and Malcolm McLaren overheard this. Later, he'd gone outside, got talking to a bloke ... 'Sex Pistols, inside, do you want to come and see them?' This bloke says no, I'm waiting to meet someone. Malcolm said, 'Are you the bass player?' He said yes. 'Oh, they're inside.' He came in and said, 'Here's your new bass player' and I met Steve Diggle. He was actually waiting to meet a completely different bloke, because about five minutes later, Malcolm came in with somebody else saying, 'It's your guitarist.' Never saw him again. I went up and I started talking to Steve and he'd just discovered the errors of his ways. He'd actually replied to another advert for lead guitarist but ended up with me instead. So I said, 'Right, well, while you're here why don't you see the band. We're trying to do stuff like that.' So he liked it, so we arranged that he would come over to Howard's rehearsal place the next day. He was a bass player and he had a bass guitar, it was perfect – it was like he fell out of the sky.

Devoto and Shelley were the only ones at the Lesser Free Trade Hall who had actually seen the Pistols play live before. For everyone else, there were few expectations other than the promise of an unusual name.

MALCOLM MCLAREN: You were never looking to hopefully see a good rock and roll band, you were looking and hoping to see the most dreadful and wonderful ... energy ... that could be best described as your first fuck really.

PETER OLDHAM (audience member): We thought, right, yeah, we'll have some of that. So we went down into this little church-hall type set up, no stage lighting ... just a little concept band on.

IAIN GREY (audience member): When we got there, on the door there's this guy who totally freaked me out. One-piece leather outfit, a Space Age teddy boy. He was Malcolm McLaren and he just looked so cool. He was saying to us, 'Oh don't come in yet, the support band are on at the moment and they're crap. Come back in half an hour.' I felt old. He was, like, ten years older than me and he was so cool.

EDDIE GARRITY: Yeah, well I went with Iain, he used to be a devotee of the *NME*. He'd read in there that this new thing was happening. I wasn't really into it at all, that sort of paper. He said, there's something really big going to be happening in Manchester and we've got to be there. So I went along with him.

MARK E. SMITH (lead singer: The Fall): We met up in a pub round the corner, Cox's Bar. We were all going, shall we go, shan't we go? Sounds a bit naff to me, it's from London. It had to be American for us. Malcolm McLaren walked into the pub – into the vault – and he had this leather suit on … big ginger hair … winkle pickers. Pretty unusual in those days. He came over to us and said, 'Are you coming over to see the band?' It really impressed me – a good management style that. Impressive. So we decided to go. And it was good.

PETER HOOK: The way they were dressed was absolutely bizarre, Malcolm McLaren being dressed in leather in the ticket booth, giving out tickets as you walked in. Then he came and sat at the end of our row. I'd never seen anybody bloody dressed in leather. I'd seen Alvin Stardust on telly, but I'd never seen anything like that in my life.

TONY WILSON: My memories were Malcolm wearing black leather trousers, and a black leather jacket. Years later, I discovered that this whole thing had been to sell leather trousers.

ALAN HEMPSHALL: We arrived in good time and just scurried straight to the front. It was a seated auditorium

IAN MOSS: I ended up going on my own. I phoned various girls up to see if they wanted to go, but just the name 'Sex Pistols' seemed to put them off.

JORDAN: It was very weird because you never knew what was going to happen, you'd turn up somewhere and people didn't know who the Sex Pistols were and they'd just come in to see a gig. You'd get a bad reception and you know it was very ground breaking. People were amazed and blown away by it. But on the other hand, a lot of people travelled. A lot of fans travelled to see every gig. It's almost like they knew it was going to be … history. We got a load of fans that were really very well known.

Punk muse and original Pistols fan Jordan, as seen on Granada TV's
So It Goes in 1976

TONY WILSON: All I knew was ... Lesser Free Trade
Hall ... this band the Sex Pistols. I didn't know the
Buzzcocks were meant to play or anything. I didn't even
know the Buzzcocks didn't exist at that point in my life.
All I knew is that Howard Trafford/Devoto had sent me
the tape. The person I actually talked to at the gig was the
geezer in black leather trousers and the black leather
jacket, which was Mr McLaren, who said hello to me and I
said hello to him.

PETE SHELLEY: I knew of him (Wilson) because I used
to watch him on TV every night. I don't know ... I've no
strong recollection of him being at the first one. I don't
actually remember him coming up to the box office saying,
'I'm on the guest list, or anything like that. It would fit

more that he would be at the second one rather than the first.

HOWARD DEVOTO: Whether he (Wilson) actually came to that one, I don't know. I don't think he'd make it up. I think whatever he says is probably the truth.

TONY WILSON: It's confusing as to who was there. Certainly Morrisey (The Smiths) was there. Steven was the little writer kid, the little intellectual at the back. He was a friend of McLaren's because of his fondness for The New York Dolls. This is Steven Morrisey, probably aged about fifteen. I'm pretty sure Hucknall (Mick – Simply Red) was there. I think at least two members of Joy Division were there. I think Mark E. Smith (The Fall) was there.

ALAN HEMPSALL: I would say thirty to fifty people, tops, were there. The only person that I can say for sure was there is Tony Wilson, because I actually spoke to him. I spoke to him because I'd met him at Kiss the month before at the Free Trade Hall, the big hall downstairs they'd played in May.

TONY WILSON: I think when things happen, everyone claims to have been there, so I mean, normal activity really. If some guy says he saw me there and we talked about the Kiss gig that's probably very correct actually. Because we (Granada TV) had just done the Kiss concert about two months earlier, an hysterical concert that was in the main auditorium. I presume a lot of people who went to the second (Sex Pistols) gig claim to have been at the first gig. I think that's where it gets confused. I mean we now say thirty or forty, could have been more like twenty. It was absolutely empty. I think a lot of people who went to the second gig claim to have been at the first gig. I was on holiday for the second gig.

HOWARD DEVOTO: The only people, apart from Pete (Shelley), myself, Steve Diggle and all the Pistols crew that I'd be reasonably certain were there were Paul Morley and Morrisey, he (Morrisey) wrote a letter to the *NME* about the gig (describing it as 'a front parlour affair').

TONY WILSON: Doesn't matter who was there ... just the fact there was enough people there.

HOWARD DEVOTO: I think the Lesser Free Trade Hall held about four hundred. We had made the tickets, we had actually hand-crafted those tickets and numbered them. So I think that figure of a hundred is probably as accurate as anybody could come up with. It did not feel full – there's no way around that – and it was seated. And up until right at the end, people stayed seated.

As the audience took their seats, there was disappointment in some areas that the tantalisingly named Buzzcocks were a no-show. The band on stage, though, were going down pretty well. And Howard's holiday-job friend Geoff was going down a storm.

ALAN HEMPSALL: It was weird because there was a band on. The tickets quite clearly say 'Buzzcocks'. Anyway, this band came on stage and as rock bands liked to have in the Seventies, they had their name on the bass drum and it was Solstice. They performed a set of probably around thirty forty minutes of their own stuff, with one or two rock standards. My abiding memory of the support group is that the singer had a droopy moustache, but he was also sporting a love bite on his neck. They did this absolutely faithful version of 'Nantucket Sleighride' by Mountain (keyboard-dominated US rock band who played at the Woodstock festival in 1969). It was the theme tune of the political television programme, which you might remember called *Weekend World*.

GLEN MATLOCK: Right, well I like Mountain ... See, the thing is, I was more than likely in Tommy Ducks (a popular Manchester pub which displayed a collection of female customers' underwear pinned to the ceiling) when they was on.

PETER SHELLEY: We always used to take them (Sex Pistols) to Tommy Ducks. They liked Tommy Ducks because they stuck ladies underwear up on the ceiling and they thought that was amazing. So every time they came and said, 'Lets go to Tommy Ducks!'

JORDAN: I remember Pete Shelley taking me to Tommy Ducks. It's pub where there's all these knickers on the ceiling. There's no other time I would have been taken there, so I guess I must have been there. Yeah, I swear I was there!

Sadly, Tommy Ducks is no longer there; it was demolished some years later.

HOWARD DEVOTO: I don't recall seeing anybody that I thought, 'There's a punk'. Pete and I had changed our look considerably and got very curious looks from the Teds in Piccadilly (central square in Manchester). I don't really recall anybody at that gig looking like a punk, it was a mostly male audience looking like Manchester males did in those days.

EDDIE GARRITY: Well I remember there wasn't really

a lot of people there. You know there was a lot of hype about it in the paper, I remember seeing the article in the paper, this was going to be the next big thing. And we got there, expecting to see a massive crowd. There was no queues or anything and some really scruffy git on the door. It was 50p or something daft. Just go upstairs into this empty hall.

PETER HOOK: The Sex Pistols were supported by a group that played a twenty-minute version of 'Nantucket Sleighride'. They were old, complete dyed-in-the-wool, Deep Purple/ Led Zeppelin-type rockers. I remember there were very, very few people there. About forty or something. I went with Bernard (Sumner, later of Joy Division/New Order) and his wife.

PAUL MORLEY: They played a load of cover versions of songs by the Allman Brothers or Mountain or Man. There was this fantastic Welsh group called Man who were like the British Grateful Dead and they had an album called *Be Good To Yourself At Least Once A Day*, that came with a free fold-up map of Wales. They did this song called "I like to eat Bananas because they've got no bones ... I like Marijuana because it gets me stoned" ... Being a Man fan, I was aware that this group was doing it and I thought this was pretty good, fantastic, how great is that?

HOWARD DEVOTO: I think they (Solstice) had a strobe light, one of those you'd have seen in your local pub. You'd have thought they were pretty good, actually. But, they were not the right vibe at all really. But, what the hell. A few people clapped. They weren't booed off or anything like that.

Howard Devoto, real name Howard Trafford, the driving force
behind the Pistols' Manchester gigs (Photo: Peter Oldham)

PAUL MORLEY: The first Sex Pistols show, I went on my
own, and my memory of it really is that everyone was just
sort of very polite ... and the fact that we were seated. And
there weren't many people there. It seemed, because of the
smallness of the venue and yet it was seated, a little bit
like something you might come across in your school, like
some kind of weird assembly or something.

I wrote about it instantly for a fanzine I was doing and
I've described everybody there as like furry freaks or plastic posers. I still had long hair and I believe some form of
facial hair. I think I just got the feeling that everybody
watched it with a kind of strange trepidation. We just
didn't know what the heck was about to happen and that
was further encouraged by the fact that the support group
were a bunch of furry freaks. They were a bunch of heavy
metal kind of guys in flared denim – the whole thing that

obviously was actually being wrenched away by the Sex Pistols.

IAN MOSS: The support band worried me. They were just another typical rock band playing rock music. I thought, 'Have I wasted a Friday night here? Are the Sex Pistols just going to be another version of this?' That was what people were used to seeing, it was disappointing. They probably got a nice round of applause for their efforts. It certainly wasn't memorable.

PETER OLDHAM: Very polite applause at first and then they came on with 'Nantucket Sleighride'. Everybody was quite keen on that one. They shovelled off and then the main act came on.

HOWARD DEVOTO: Pete and I saw the Sex Pistols when they were supporting Screaming Lord Sutch. The second night we saw them they were supporting Mr Big. These were the standard acts you would get on the college circuit. Solstice were no different. There just weren't the groups to put together punk gigs at that time. That thing in the Lesser Free Trade Hall was among the first punk gigs.

PAUL MORLEY: Of course they were the inappropriate group to have, but in another sense they lulled us into a false sense of security and made what was about to happen even more dramatic.

PETER OLDHAM: It was more a matter of everybody turning up in cheesecloth and flared trousers. There was no such thing (as punk) in Manchester. I suppose you could say Slaughter and the Dogs were at it somewhere.

HOWARD DEVOTO: Longish hair, I don't know, duffel coats. Paul Morley always looked like Francis Rossi out of Status Quo to me, with his long hair. They (the audience) would have all looked like Solstice fans

PAUL MORLEY: Unfortunately he's very, very accurate. You know, I didn't even get my hair cut for the second Sex Pistols gig. The next time they played, Johnny Rotten wouldn't talk to me. He actually said, 'I ain't talking to you, you look like a student.' That was the moment I got my hair cut. I went home and cut it with blunt scissors and ended up looking probably more like Rod Stewart. But at the time at least it took me away from the Francis Rossi area.

IAN MOSS: I've a horrible feeling that I was wearing a beige suit.

TONY WILSON: There was this old-fashioned little theatre, with a very high proscenium stage and about thirty or forty of us, sitting separately in these seats. I was on my own. We all sat there and ... my prime memory is of me being like that (*pulls startled face*) and I think everyone else was just like that (*pulls startled face again*) ... shocked.

IAIN GREY: Johnny Rotten ambled on ... and that was like just a shock. He was one of the most frightening people I'd ever seen at that time ... this lad with a thousand yard stare, just stood there. And then he started playing ... and it was as though he was just staring at me. He was probably just looking out to the audience.

PAUL MORLEY: He meant it, man ... . and you felt that more than anything you'd ever come across before. That he was really living it out and that, at the time, was quite unusual and completely refreshing. We've lost it again now, so it still seems to have a real kind of potency, even though it was rock music, it was absolutely expressing something deep and important to himself and you kind of got that, rather than any individual sense of the songs.

ALAN HEMPSALL: The Sex Pistols came on and they looked as you remember them from loads of press photographs. John Rotten had a tee-shirt with the word 'TITS' emblazoned in sequins. They had these thick brothel creepers on. My friend who's sat right next to me, he's a bit of a wag. He shouts out, 'You're not very sexy are you?'

IAN MOSS: I think the audience were sat there waiting to be impressed ... or disappointed. So the attitude was coming from the stage and almost exclusively from Johnny Rotten ... just the way he moved, the way he sounded, the little asides between songs. It was just not like some preening rock star, it was a completely different performance to any I'd ever seen and I'd seen hundreds of bands. Completely different.

PAUL MORLEY: You could stare into the whites of his eyes. It was terrifying and addictive. It was fantastic. The Sex Pistols coming to Manchester is interesting because they didn't go to Liverpool and they didn't go to Glasgow or Sheffield.

PETER OLDHAM: They played 'Pretty Vacant'. It was ... intimidation on legs. These guys came out and, 'Bang!' It was there.

TONY WILSON: Then you begin to understand what they were doing ... just playing ridiculously fast, and just putting loads of energy into it. It was absolutely real ... everything else was unreal. It's been five, six, seven years since one had encountered anything real – on stage – in music. It was real, it was completely not obvious what it was – heaven knows what it was – it's just, oh God ... I've been waiting for this. God, it's real.

PAUL MORLEY: You kind of thought, oh this is interesting, there's thirty or forty other people that are clearly interested in newness. You just kind of half acknowledged that there was other kind of strange people interested in this new music but you had no idea who they were, nobody I'd even recognise going to other concerts at the Manchester Free Trade Hall. They just popped out fresh, so you just get this vague feeling of people milling about in a slightly transfixed sense.

A bootleg of the gig reveals that the Pistols played 'Don't Gimme Me No Lip Child', 'I Did You No Wrong', 'Substitute', 'No Feelings' and 'Pretty Vacant'. 'Submission' is introduced as 'a pop song'. There is a great deal of shouting from the audience. 'Get off, you're crap!' one audience member cries. 'Got a lot of mouth, sat there in the dark,' Rotten declares. 'If you don't like it, fuck off out of it,' he says, before the band launch into 'What'cha Gonna Do About it?' by the Small Faces. Glen Matlock can be heard, quite clearly, doing harmonies to accompany Rotten's lead vocal. They play 'No Fun' twice after failing to agree with the crowd on what they should do by way of an encore. Rotten even offers to play some Osmonds. 'This is dying a death,' says Rotten from the stage. If, as many people have stated, there are only a few dozen there, then they are a very noisy few dozen indeed. It backs up Devoto's belief that there was nearer to a hundred people there. Towards the end, with people clearly out of their seats, Rotten wonders where everyone has come from.

IAN MOSS: Quite late into the gig, there was a bit of banter from the audience to the stage. They were shouting out the names of bands. You know, 'The 13th Floor Elevators! What do you think of them?' Then somebody shouted, 'Eddie and the Hot Rods!' and Rotten looked and he said, 'Our imitators ... '

PAUL MORLEY: It was erotically charged, the whole thing was erotic. You know, the funny thing is they could play really well. Amongst the more 'pseud' of us, that was something that was important . It wasn't a shambles at all, they were very powerful and they had all the right moves. I just remember at that first show, really being in a kind of state of shock almost. I was quite still, absorbing it all. What a kind of remarkable revolution had happened within a music that still used guitars and covered The Who and the Small Faces, it was still obvious reference points. It was still rock and roll, it was very much about that ... but all the sexiness you wanted from the music and the anger and the power. It just seemed to be condensed into it and I just was transfixed by it.

PETER HOOK: The band played really well. Johnny Rotten had his own unique style of singing ... Everybody thought they were rubbish, it was down to the sound guy – it's really the sound guy that's responsible for me thinking I could form a band. If you listen to the bootleg, they're actually playing quite well. I mean they were quite an established rhythm section, Paul Cook and Matlock. Steve Jones could actually play guitar. It was so aggressive and it was that that actually turned you on.

TONY WILSON: Steve Jones (Sex Pistol guitarist) was wearing a boiler suit and his entire act was a Pete Townshend impersonation.

IAN MOSS: Johnny Rotten had this kind of ratty pullover on. You could see the cigarette burns on his arm. A lot of people in hindsight say to me what we liked about them was they were rubbish but they didn't sound rubbish to me, they sounded magnificent. They patently *could* play. It was rudimentary, but it was tight.

GLEN MATLOCK: We were supposed to have short hair and its a surprise quite how long our hair was. It does look quite tame in comparison to what punks were supposed to look like. But we never saw ourselves as a punk band. We hated the term punk: we were the Sex Pistols.

TONY WILSON: They did 'Stepping Stone' by The Monkees and suddenly you go, oh wow ... I get it ... fine. But it was basically sitting with your mouth open, thinking, 'Good heavens'. It happened again for me, thirteen years later in the Hacienda. The first time it happened, the first time you see rock and roll die ... and then be reborn, you just think, 'Oh my God, what is this?' The next time round its like, 'Aah ... been here before, isn't this wonderful?' At the time I think I had my mouth open. I was probably swallowing fucking flies.

PAUL MORLEY: The kind of rock music that you'd loved over the years, like Led Zeppelin and The Who ... the Rolling Stones .... that seemed a little bit before your time. The Pistols brought everything bang up to date; it was absolutely for you. It was about the times. You couldn't really get any idea what they were singing about, but you just had a gut instinct that this was about how you felt. And about the nation. And about how pissed off you were. And about what you were expected to accept as a teenager. And about how fucked up your future was going to be. You just knew that's what it was all about even with the mayhem that was being caused. It was nothing to do with pop music in that sense; it was much more than that. It was a big bizarre philosophy being thrown at you and that was incredibly exciting.

PETER HOOK: It was absolutely bizarre. It was the most shocking thing I've ever seen in me life, it was just unbelievable. And the sound was terrible. We just looked at each other and thought 'My God!' They looked like they were having such a fantastic time. It was so ... alien to everything. You just thought, 'God, we could do that.' And I still to this day can't imagine why on Earth we thought we could do that, because I'd never played a musical instrument.

PETE SHELLEY: They were excellent. They made all the hairs on the back of your neck stand up.

EDDIE GARRITY: Well they were just dreadful ... that first gig, totally unrehearsed. I think they'd just gone out of the way to get noticed and be as bad as they possibly could be.

TONY WILSON: Most of pop music – and most of rock and roll – is not real. The guys are just people, just playing guitars or singing, because they're good at it and it sounds good. That isn't rock and roll. That isn't pop music. Pop music and rock and roll is when someone means it, when it's real. For me personally, academically, it wasn't until about the seventh number. They did all these other numbers and the seventh number was 'Stepping Stone'. You can imagine Johnny singing and suddenly there's a song that you knew, being done by this bunch of maniacs.

HOWARD DEVOTO: It wasn't chaotic or anything like that. (Prior to the gig) the Sex Pistols had gone out for a drink with one of my philosophy lecturers, a wonderful man by the name of Mr David Melling. Nice gentleman, of great bearing and dignity. They all went out for a drink in the pub over the road. It's one of those events in one's life ... I would really like to have been there. They all got on very well and David assured me that they were very nice lads. It's just one of those things where two parts of your life come together and you think, 'My goodness me, there's an existential happening!'

PETER OLDHAM: It was more like the audience reaction in *The Producers* (film featuring the song 'Springtime for Hitler') The audience sat there with their mouths open. After they finished, they weren't quite sure whether they were good or what. But the attack and the aggression of it was something to behold.

MALCOLM MCLAREN: I can only remember that those kids were believing that they were at the beginning of something. And they believed they had in their reach something authentic. And they were not going to ever let that go. A rare jewel ... like a ruby in a field of tin.

GLEN MATLOCK: So I'm told. And I know people who were at the gig. But I mean, when you're in a band you kind of get taken to where you're going ... and what happens when you get there is not totally within your hands

PETER HOOK: Well the funny thing was, I wasn't involved in music. I didn't know anybody that was. There was about forty, fifty people (at the gig) ... if that. I didn't know anybody. I didn't know anybody in the musical circle in Manchester. But there was nobody that I knew there, apart from Bernard (Sumner), his wife and Terry Mason, who was a guy that I used to go to school with. I don't remember if Ian Curtis (Joy Division) was there. I can't remember if he was there or not.

PETER OLDHAM: I couldn't guess really, probably about fiftyish. Probably along that line.

IAN MOSS: I personally would have thought there'd be about seventy or eighty people there.

TONY WILSON: So who does claim to have been there properly on that first night? Who do we know was there? Hooky and Bernard were there.

HOWARD DEVOTO: I understand some of them – because they became Joy Division eventually – were there. I mean, they weren't people I knew, so I just I wouldn't know at all. I'd only be really confident about Paul Morley and Morrisey. I think. There's a big dispute as to how many people were there that evening. I personally think there were about a hundred people there.

PETE SHELLEY: There's a lot of unanswered questions about those gigs – might have been something in the beer, I don't know.

TONY WILSON: It shows the wonderfulness of the event, the fact that the capacity is only about a hundred and fifty at the Lesser Free Trade Hall ... seven and a half thousand people claim to have been there. It's what happens at wonderful events. It's always the same. People just think they went there. I feel very privileged ... being there ... sitting there ... and gawping. Very strange.

PETER OLDHAM: I was quite impassioned about it at

the time. It was pretty good. There was no stage lighting, the sound was pretty poor. But it was just the actual attack of the band, it had a spark to it.

TONY WILSON: As I walked out, this geezer in the black leather goes, 'What did you think of that Mr Wilson?' I said, 'Well Malcolm, I think ... Yeah! But the Pete Townshend stuff ... ' He says, 'Yeah, yeah, I know, it's going, it's going.'

IAIN GREY: Got home, got all my shirts out, ripped the arms off them, got rid of my flares in the bin, this was when we got back from the gig. Me and Eddie were like, right, scrap all the songs, three minutes, three chords. It was just so exciting, the sheer presence of the band with Rotten. Everything I believed in about music up to that point was destroyed and rightfully so. This is the way. Sod all the Roxy Music, David Bowie; they actually meant something to me, something tangible that I could do, I could be like that, not where you've got to be in the audience. And I thought, I can do that. It was absolutely fantastic – a life changing event. I was eighteen at the time.

PAUL MORLEY: When you came out, you knew something had happened and your body felt hot and your blood was racing and your mind was racing. But it never occurred to you that there would be any future for it. It never occurred to you that maybe every single person in that room would go on and form bands and do whatever they did. It never occurred to you because that never happened before. It never occurred to you that anything fantastic could come from Manchester. It never occurred to you that, even though the thing we'd just seen was so fantastic, that it would inspire us to do things. It was just a fantastic experience and then, much to your surprise a few days later, you found out it was going to happen again.

IAN MOSS: The only people I spoke to were on the bus going home. There were a couple of guys on the same bus who lived in Denton I'd never seen before, but I'd seen them on the first show and they'd seen me. Their reaction was much the same as mine, and like many people from that time, without becoming close friends, it is something that's bonded us.

HOWARD DEVOTO: The Pistols, John in particular, were obviously quite pleased with the reaction they got. When they did their encore he said something to the crowd like, 'Where did you all come from?' in a not unfriendly way. Malcolm said to me afterwards something like, 'Let's do it again, let's book this again'. They felt it was definitely a success, lets do it again. Great ... okay! I book the Hall again – the Hall were very happy to have the booking again, thirty quid. So it was duly booked for about six weeks on from then. July 20.

PETER SHELLEY: They turned up, played ... there was a good turn out, I mean they were enthusiastic. So we thought, well, let's do it again.

MALCOLM MCLAREN: We were asked to return a second time and play with the so-called group, which I think Howard called the Buzzcocks.

PAUL MORLEY: The first show you just got the feeling that the Sex Pistols could have disappeared overnight and it would have been one of those things. But with the second show you knew that this was something titanic.

63

PETE SHELLEY: The whole idea was that you couldn't do such things as put on your own gigs. It was like meddling with forces beyond your control ... agents and promoters knew far better. But really it's a load of rubbish. All they do is just phone the hall, book it, get a PA in, just an afternoon's worth of phone calls and a bit of persistence and you too can be a promoter. So then the idea was to do another one, so July 20 was the second.

TONY WILSON: We were dry kindling, just absolutely ready to explode into fire that moment. Which was Devoto's doing, to put that incendiary bomb, let alone a spark into this community that is Manchester. People that were at the second gig, claim to be at the first gig, whatever, doesn't matter. What's important is, the Pistols happened.

HOWARD DEVOTO: Within weeks, well certainly by the time Buzzcocks played some four months later or so ... I got a sticky inkling that my life had changed. I certainly know I felt a whole lot different in myself, a whole lot better in myself. Suddenly I was engaged in something that really, really interested me.

Over the space of two hours, Geoff's band Solstice had ushered out the old and the Sex Pistols had ushered in the new. 1976 was summed up in the gap between Solstice finishing their set and the Pistols starting theirs. At the Lesser Free Trade in Manchester on June 4, the distance between the band and the audience had shrunk. The idea that being in a band was a calling that only a few could aspire to had been debunked. The possibility of doing 'it' yourself ... whatever that 'it' might be ... was temptingly close. Not bad for a bunch of Small Faces and Stooges cover versions. It's fortunate that the audience didn't take Rotten's advice and 'fuck off out of it', otherwise they would have missed something quite extraordinary.

3: How to Play Rock and Roll Bass Guitar

IN WHICH MR SHELLEY AND MR DEVOTO NARROWLY
AVOID A SOUND THRASHING.

*AFTER THE Lesser Free Trade Hall gig, the Pistols carried on
with the rather haphazard live performance schedule that
was becoming increasingly their norm. They played the 100
Club, London, as their next concert, the fifth time they'd
played the Oxford Street venue. In the meantime, there
was a flurry of activity in Manchester.*

*Just as important to the shape of rock as the first and
second gigs at the Lesser Free Trade Hall in 1976, was the
gap in between the two. There was organisation. There
were plans. Young men who had not managed to get their
'shit together' for the first gig, got their 'shit together' very
quickly indeed. A small but noisy scattering of long-hairs at
the first gig was building up to be a serious crowd for the
second.*

TONY WILSON: Maybe it's only in a small city that you
have that kind of communication, that can take you from
thirty-five people on June 4 to several hundred on July 20.
The word goes out, the word spreads.

PETER HOOK: I think the people that saw the first Sex Pistols gig – in the same way that we did – walked out of it, did something and then went and told whoever they knew about it and it just came on from there. So by the time you got to the second one there were more bands than soft mick. There was literally forty, sixty, eighty, a hundred bands. Everybody was forming a band

For me, it changed, literally, the next day. It was overnight and I went round telling everybody I knew about the Sex Pistols.

IAN MOSS: I was evangelical about it, honestly. I told everybody about that band, everybody I encountered, about the Sex Pistols

PAUL MORLEY: I've no idea of the time difference between the first and the second show, but I just get the feeling that we'd all run around and said, 'You've got to come, you've got to come, this is amazing, they're actually playing.' And by then, the myth of the Sex Pistols had got bigger and it was clearly a more obviously dramatic thing that was happening. Whereas I got the feeling the first thing was almost on the quiet … there was almost like a rumour of a rumour when they came that first time. Clearly very obscure, although the *NME* was writing about them. The whole power of the Pistols myth was beginning to happen and the Pistols themselves already looked like something had happened to them. You got the feeling that the second time they were beginning to change physically and mentally and they knew they were part of something and that energy was transmitted a lot more the second time than the first time.

PETE SHELLEY: I suppose it ended up being a different kind of following. People, instead of just being passive observers of the culture, became active participants and started forming their own bands. Just doing basically what they were doing anyway ... but more accelerated. I think it was the fact that nobody was stopping them doing it.

PETER HOOK: It was that immediate; it was like somebody opening ... a door in a darkened room

TONY WILSON: I was a big Van Morrison fan, but afterwards I'd gone to visit an old girlfriend in London. She said, 'What do you think of the new Van Morrison album?' and I'd go, pardon? Who cares? The world has turned, it's all moved on, the most wonderful moment grows from that single spark.

IAIN GREY: Going to see the Pistols, that was the catalyst. Suddenly, overnight. we thought right, tear the sleeves off our shirts, this is it. Overnight, the arms came off the shirts and the drainpipes and you know, 'Get your hair cut.'

PETER HOOK: Literally the next day, I went to Mazel's in Manchester and bought a bass guitar for thirty-five quid. (Mazel Radio was a music/electrical secondhand shop near Manchester's Piccadilly train station). I went in and I went, 'Can I have a bass guitar?' and he went, 'Well, here's one. Thirty-five quid.' Give him thirty-five quid and walked out with the guitar and thought, what the bloody hell am I going to do with this? So I went to a music shop on Deansgate and bought a book on how to play rock and roll bass guitar: *Play in a Day*.

Peter Hook immediately set about the business of 'rehearsing' with his friend – and later band-mate in Joy Division and New Order – Bernard Sumner.

PETER HOOK: We didn't have an amp. Bernard wired up his Gran's gramophone with four wires connecting my bass guitar and his guitar to her gramophone ... and we played through that. She went mad when she came home, we'd ruined her gramophone. She went crazy.

Elsewhere, another enticing possibility was underway: that of putting the Pistols on television. Two hundred yards away from the Lesser Free Trade Hall is Granada Television and that's where the plot was being hatched.

TONY WILSON: The night after I saw the Pistols, I went running to my boss and said, 'Chris, Chris, saw this band last night, got to have them on,' ... fantastic, fantastic, screaming shouting ... 'Doesn't matter that they're not signed, they're fantastic', blah, blah, blah. Chris Pye (producer, *So It Goes*) wasn't having any of this. So he said, 'Right, well you've got to take Malcolm Clarke, your researcher, who is a responsible human being – not like you – take him to see the band and we'll see what he thinks.'

CHRIS PYE: Tony came through he door and said, 'Hey man! I saw this great gig ... ' Tony didn't describe things in detail most of the time. Tony just came in with a kind of wave of enthusiasm. It's the enthusiasm that drove us really.

PETER WALKER: All I can remember is that from a very early stage in the series, perhaps episode one of the whole series, Tony Wilson decided that he wanted to try and get a group like the Sex Pistols on the show ... because that was more of what he saw the future of music was going to be.

Apart from the stuff we were getting on which was very fringey, obviously, because there were other programmes that did the mainstream music and we always tried to make sure that it was always good music.

TONY WILSON: All that summer, it was the last great heat wave. It's really weird to think that punk, with its heatwave boredom and industrial mentality, came in that fantastic summer. So on a fantastically hot, wonderful, sunny afternoon, we drove to Walthamstow (in London) and parked outside about eight o'clock, bright wonderful blue sky. We walked into this massive civic hall that was completely dark and kind of quite cool. At the far end, this racket was coming off the stage and you could see about twenty people, that was all, in like a semi-circle. As we got nearer, the reason it was a semi-circle was that that was the gobbing distance. John (Johnny Rotten) was like gobbing as hard as he could, so that's why this little audience of about twenty-five people were just out of gobbing range. And they were stunning.

JORDAN: Its very difficult to say exactly why the Pistols were so strong. The only thing I can think is that very rarely do you get a bunch of people that come together, that just make a unit and all have the same attitude. Quite often, things are very pre-conceived, especially these days, they're very much a product of producers and managers.

GLEN MATLOCK: We went everywhere just to get some gigs, just to get a bit of stagecraft together. We played this Conservative club once, and we're hammering away and a guy kept coming in to tell us to turn it down a little bit. And a little bit more. And in the end he said, 'No good lads, we'll pay you, but you'll just have to stop because they can't hear the bingo in the next room.'

JORDAN: One of my funniest occasions was when the Pistols were playing the Pier at Hastings, which is right on the south coast of England. There's a little sort of domed area at the back of the Pier which usually some organist would be playing in the summer season. Malcolm had got them booked in there and Sid (Vicious, not then in the band) and I went down by train to see the Pistols on this pier. Nearly the whole audience were German, Italian and Swedish tourists all down there for their summer hols. It was absolutely bizarre.

PAUL MORLEY: I was doing a fanzine at that time. I'd started to put it together before I'd seen the Pistols and the Ramones and Patti Smith. So it had Dylan in it, and it had T-Rex in it and it had Ted Nugent. I had to change very quickly in mid flow. It still had Bob Dylan on the cover, because I'd printed a lot of it and I'd paid for it, so I couldn't afford to re-do it, but very quickly I rammed in a little bit about the Pistols and a bit about the Stranglers. Now I don't know which one I reviewed, I get a feeling I reviewed the first one but I don't know, unfortunately. I was young. I didn't put much detail into the review, which I wish I had done now.

PETER HOOK: I was wearing a dog collar and having my hair spiked up and wearing army boots. People literally would stop in the street and trip over. You'd be putting soap in your hair to make it stick up. Me and Bernard (Sumner) used to go to buy Scout shirts and paint swastikas on them and put SS badges on and all that crap. God, you wouldn't be allowed anywhere near it now! It was funny.

The focus for Howard Devoto and Pete Shelley was to ensure they actually made it on to the bill of the July 20 gig. As the date approached, another band was added to the bill, above the Buzzcocks. Wayne Barrett, Mike Rossi, Howard Bates and Mad Muffet were a bunch of glam rock toughs from the biggest housing estate in Europe. Slaughter and the Dogs had broken out of south Manchester and got a gig in the city centre – a very big deal at the time.

WAYNE BARRETT (lead singer Slaughter and the Dogs): All there was to do was hang around the chippy, go round on your push bike, a lot of people robbing, silly things like that. Nothing. Mike (Rossi) and myself, we'd go down to

The kids from the council estate: Mick Rossi (left) and Wayne Barrett of Slaughter and the Dogs supporting the Pistols, July 20, 1976 (Photo: Peter Oldham)

73

the press factory when they distributed all the newspapers, like four, five in the morning, to pick up the *New Musical Express*, *Sounds* and everything. That filled us in with the Pistols information and things like that.

Slaughter and the Buzzcocks were chalk and cheese – and grated against each other immediately. The first thing the college boys did was check out the competition from the council estate kids.

HOWARD DEVOTO: I tended to be the one on the blower, but Pete was helping out all along, getting the group together, organising the gig, going along to check out Slaughter and the Dogs. We did travel out to Wythenshawe and saw them play. Slaughter and the Dogs turned out to be kind of Bowie and Roxy kids.

WAYNE BARRETT: They came to my Mum's place. I always remember my mum was scared to death when she saw Pete Shelley all dressed up and everything.

PETE SHELLEY: They (Slaughter and the Dogs) always used to think they were the best. We knew that *thinking* that you're the best doesn't necessarily mean you *are* the best. So we were more philosophical about the dispute. As a result they saw us as being rivals, and as a result lost the plot completely.

WAYNE BARRETT: Everybody we met, they said, 'Where are you playing next?' We just said, 'We're playing in the Lesser Free Trade Hall.' So they said, 'When?' And we gave them the information.

Slaughter had already been making noises south of the city as they went about the business of getting themselves noticed. Something which they proved to be remarkably adept at.

TONY WILSON: Martin Hannett, the young Manchester nascent genius producer who I'd begun to know, insisted that I go to a gig in 'The Shed' I think it was called, in Portwood in Stockport on May 15, 1976 – this is two and a half weeks before the Pistols – to see a band called Slaughter and the Dogs. It was weird, a bit Bowie-esque ... wearing dresses and playing vacuum cleaners. It was weird and it was different and it wasn't like any of that crap that we were putting out, you know, John Miles and Be-Bop Deluxe, just technically nice music.

PETE SHELLEY: Me and Howard were grammar school boys, so it wasn't really the sound of the terraces. I mean, me and Howard read books and things like that, you know.

MICK ROSSI (guitarist Slaughter and the Dogs): We went to Sharston High School.

I interviewed Mick Rossi and Wayne Barrett together. They are a double act. Rossi is small in stature and as piss-thin as he was twenty-five years ago. Barrett is well-fed and beefy. When reading this, be aware that Rossi now speaks with a strong American accent. When I asked him to identify himself for the tape, he replied: 'Mick Rossi – guitar player and full-time dreamer.' Wayne Barrett, his 'other half' has retained his Mancunian twang. Their act is funnier if you read it in your head with those accents in mind.

WAYNE BARRETT: I was in music school doing music lessons. I was playing bass at that time. I met up with Mike in the schoolyard. After that we started hanging out together and then we decided to start a band off ... dreams of Bowie, Roxy Music, Alice Cooper, Slade ... all the Seventies glam stuff. We were told at school by our headmaster, Mr Muscott, if you're still alive and still kicking ...

MICK ROSSI: Jesus, a blast from the past.

WAYNE BARRETT: ... he got us into his room once and he said to us that we'd all end on the dole. Or in prison. And we wouldn't ever work..

MICK ROSSI: That's encouragement for you, right?

WAYNE BARRETT: If you're in school and somebody says that to you ... what do you want us to do, kill ourselves? We just said, 'We're going make something out of ourselves,' and that pushed us on.

MICK ROSSI: We used to rehearse in his (Barrett's) mum's front room. We'd take the budgie cage off and then the stand became the mike stand. I had a shitty little guitar, so we kind of bummed around doing that for a little bit.

WAYNE BARRETT: The first band was called Wayne Barrett and the Mind Troop.

MICK ROSSI: There was nothing, literally nothing, in Wythenshawe; just Labour clubs and people singing Tom Jones impersonations. And bingo. That's how we started off, we started doing the Labour clubs as Slaughter and the Dogs and doing a whole bunch of covers. But we started writing, basically right away. That was eye-opening, doing the Labour clubs. We used to do two sets and I think we got paid fifteen quid. Which was a lot of money then. We'd all pile into the back of a van, it would be a set – and it would be the bingo which was the highlight of the evening – and then our second set.

WAYNE BARRETT: One night at a Conservative club, there was this big fat lad who introduced us: 'The Slaughtered Dog, playing here tonight.' So we went on stage to round about forty people who's average age was eighty-five. We did the four songs, and..

MICK ROSSI: Came off ...

WAYNE BARRETT: 'Look, I'll pay you ... '

MICK ROSSI: 'Go home ... sod off.'

WAYNE BARRETT: You've got to imagine the Wythenshawe situation. At that time it was like ... it was hell. Everything was unemployment, unemployment, unemployment. There was robbing all over the place. When you write a song in that kind of environment, you can't say, 'I love you, I love you, I love you.' It's got to be a little bit angry. We didn't set out to be punks.

MICK ROSSI: Before we started doing covers, we actually wrote a song called 'Love, Speed And Beer.' That was the first song we ever wrote.

WAYNE BARRETT: The punk thing, we didn't really

know what the punk thing meant. We were just banging on the guitar and yelling our heads off, basically saying, 'Listen to us.' But we were wary about what was happening in London.

MICK ROSSI: There was such a lack of activity in Manchester at the time – in terms of new bands and new blood – so anything that was coming in was great,

IAIN GREY: I used to go to school with Mick Rossi. There was one time going to a music store in Manchester. He hadn't warned me, but he had a guitar case with him – which I thought had a guitar in. So in we go, he picks up this Fender Stratocaster, puts it in the case and walks out. The woman had seen what he done and he just said to me: 'Run!' I get home, the police are at my house, Mick's buried it in his garden. He left it there for six or seven months till he thought it was safe to dig up. That's the way they were. Wythenshawe scallies

WAYNE BARRETT: We'd go into Mike's bedroom or into mine. You'd get the guitar, bash a few chords out and then get paper and a pen ... and see what happens.

Opinion on Slaughter and the Dogs has always been divided. They were either the authentic howl of council estate teen anger ... or a bunch of Glam Rock chancers out to make a buck.

TONY WILSON: To be honest, if I have to stand here and say, 'Would you rather have Slaughter and the Dogs or The Damned as the build-up to this cultural revolution?' I'd rather have Slaughter and the Dogs. I'd rather have Wythenshawe.

MICK ROSSI: We did a show at the Forum (the only major venue in Wythenshawe) and Wayne's look then ... he came on with patent decorating pants, a pair of sneakers, an old jacket with the *Guardian* in his pocket, a waistcoat, a watch and a ratty old shirt. That would be classed as punk I guess in today's terms, but it was just sort of something that happened.

EDDIE GARRITY (lead singer: Ed Banger and the Nosebleeds): I went to school with Mike and then he got expelled. He went to another school and met Wayne Barrett. So we were going to start a band before he did that (form Slaughter and the Dogs). Then later I joined them anyway. We was in a band called Wild Ram then. I think it was more the fans of each band who were more rivals. Before we went on stage the leads would be cut and things like that. We'd each go to each other's gigs to see what the other one was up to and then if there was anything good, we'd copy it.

They were like our rival band in Wythenshawe. We got together to do a gig at the Forum (theatre) and Tony Wilson off the telly came along to that one, to do the introductions. He mentioned that we were both part of this new punk movement for some reason. So obviously that's why we went to the second gig 'cause we'd already been pulled into it.

MICK ROSSI: We did the Wythenshawe Forum, which is a real big place. It was unheard of and it was promoted by our manager, so it was off our own back that we did that.

WAYNE BARRETT: If there's a fifth member of the group, its got to be Ray (Rossi, manager) because he was the real backbone of the band. He kept us together for ages, because we'd be in the rehearsal room and after the third song, we'd be beating shit out of each other basically. Because we were kids. He gave us a lot of guidance, he always had good vision. Ray did a lot, our manager.

MICK ROSSI: My brother at the time.

WAYNE BARRETT: He still is your brother.

MICK ROSSI: Hey, Ray, how you doing?

The stage was set for the next visit by the Pistols to the Lesser Free Trade Hall. Buzzcocks, for their first real gig, were bottom of the bill, with Slaughter and the Dogs on next. The Buzzcocks made some stencilled posters of their own, flagging up all three bands. Slaughter and the Dogs went to the trouble of producing their own highly profes-sional-looking, but somewhat misleading, posters. The billing has the name of the Sex Pistols underneath that of Slaughter and the Dogs.

EDDIE GARRITY: We were desperate to get on to that bill because the publicity was building for it and there was a lot of media interest in it. There was talk about getting the Buzzcocks out of the way, trying to find their address to go down and beat them up so they couldn't play. We was even going to wait outside on the night and do it but we got talked out of it (laughing). Then they said we could roadie instead so we settled for that. Ray (Rossi) was organising it so there was no point in trying to get them off the bill. Ray was pretty heavy anyway, so we left them alone.

PETE SHELLEY: Mick Rossi thought that Slaughter and the Dogs were the best band in all the world and they could get in twenty million people and sell all these tickets. They blagged Malcolm into doing the show with them as the second band.

HOWARD DEVOTO: I remember a great deal of confidence on the part of Slaughter and Dogs. A lot of front and sort of ... rubbish, really. They also produced their own posters with Slaughter and the Dogs up here (top of the poster) and Sex Pistols down there, no mention of Buzzcocks at all. Which was sweet of them. Punk was never a loving world, with everybody blissed-out together and being jolly supportive. It ain't like that in showbiz, is it?

A poster for the Pistols' second Manchester gig – with Slaughter and the Dogs topping the bill

So with cheeky posters all made up and the Buzzcocks left thankfully unmolested, there was a real buzz across the city about the second gig. There was one other indication that something was afoot after the first gig ... that something was stirring ... something was happening.

The price of entry to the Lesser Free Trade Hall to see the Sex Pistols had doubled in the space of six weeks. To £1.

4: One Up the Trouser Leg

IN WHICH THE SEX PISTOLS RETURN TO THE LESSER FREE
TRADE HALL IN THE COMPANY OF THE BUZZCOCKS AND
SLAUGHTER AND THE DOGS (SCOUNDRELS TO A MAN).

*THE SECOND SEX Pistols gig at the Lesser Free Trade Hall,
on July 20, 1976, was the culmination of the activity
sparked by the first gig. In the space of six weeks, the lads
who took the money on the door, printed the tickets and
played records during the interval had worked themselves
into the Buzzcocks, with Howard Devoto on vocals, Pete
Shelley on guitar, Steve Diggle on bass (thanks to Malcolm)
and John Maher on drums. They were bottom of the bill,
but at least they were on the bill.*

HOWARD DEVOTO: If the gig in June had been the
detonation, then that second gig was the cloud and noise
where everybody knew something was going off. It was sold
out. As far as I remember it was packed. There was a
Slaughter and the Dogs contingent. We didn't have a
contingent, apart from a few mates turning up.

Howard Devoto fronts the Buzzcocks (centre) with Steve Diggle (left)
and Pete Shelley, at the Lesser Free Trade Hall, supporting the Pistols
(photo: Peter Oldham)

TONY WILSON: July 20, I was away. I took a week's holiday in France, my first holiday for about a year. So I didn't go to the second gig. I got back and they said it was fantastic and the Buzzcocks played and there were thousands of people ... whatever.

PETE SHELLEY: For the second gig we actually made posters. We had posters made and went around and stuck them up ourselves in the middle of the night. It actually brought enough people together that they could look around and recognise each other, so the next time they met, they had that thing in common.

GARY AINSLEY (audience member): I'd sort of been into Northern Soul because I came from Oldham. There was this great idea that in the Northern Soul venues you changed into your posing gear, came out of the toilets, got onto the dance floor and performed.

LORRAINE JOYCE (audience member): We used to wear things like pencil skirts, stilettos. We used to wear straight-legged jeans, which I know now sounds absolutely nothing, but everybody was in big flares and kipper ties.

GARY AINSLEY: A friend of mine rung me up. He said, 'Do you fancy going seeing this punk band?' I said, 'What's punk?' Nobody had heard of punk. He said, They wear ripped tee-shirts' ... and as soon as he said 'ripped tee-shirts' I thought, right, I'm going. After the concert I just came out and you just knew it was just going to be so huge. You knew it was going to be. It was so different to anything.

PETER OLDHAM (audience member): There was all the A & R men dressed in jeans and carrying attaché cases, all queuing to sign them up. I think I remember seeing Tony Wilson there then. It was more of an event, there was a bit more of a buzz about it. It was gathering momentum.

WAYNE BARRETT: The gig, as it went for us, was just like doing a Labour club basically, except it was a little bit bigger and we were playing at the back of the Free Trade Hall, where we saw the big bands like Bowie, Mick Ronson.

MICK ROSSI: My hero. (Slaughter and the Dogs took part of their name from *Slaughter on Tenth Avenue*, Ronson's 1974 debut solo album. The rest of it comes from David Bowie's *Diamond Dogs* from the same year)

WAYNE BARRETT: We loved following Ronno (Mick Ronson). The punk movement, with the Pistols, we'd read about it.

MICK ROSSI: We were aware of it.

WAYNE BARRETT: We started to get pretty wary about what was happening in London.

The antagonism between Slaughter and the Dogs and the Buzzcocks was bubbling away prior to the gig.

PETE SHELLEY: They didn't sell all the tickets that they said they would. They just blagged themselves on to the bill but we bided our time. So that's why on the poster it says: Sex Pistols and Slaughter & the Dogs, not Buzzcocks.

MICK ROSSI: We had the majority of the crowd there, 'cos the first time they (the Pistols) played there, there was like thirty or so. Second time, it was packed. We had a little mob that used to follow us around, they were great.

WAYNE BARRETT: Let's say eighty percent of the people that were there, because there were a lot of people from Wythenshawe.

VANESSA CORLEY (audience member): We lived in Wythenshawe and Wayne Barrett and Slaughter and the Dogs were a Wythenshawe-based band. They played at the Forum at Wythenshawe. To then go to play at the Lesser Free Trade Hall, this was quite a big step up from the little local haunt. So that was why we went to see them.

LORRAINE JOYCE (audience member): A friend asked me to go because Slaughter and the Dogs were doing it. I'd never heard of punk, nobody knew what punk was. I said, oh yeah, I'll go. But it wasn't for me. I mean, I actually don't like punk rock. I loved the gay clubs. I loved the music in the gay clubs.

IAIN GREY (audience member): They (Slaughter and the Dogs) brought along a load of David Bowie, Roxy Music fans. So there was these punks and these Bowie/Roxy fans and there was this big fight. They were like a cabaret version of punk, Slaughter and the Dogs. They weren't credible, they were like an embarrassment. We hadn't got anywhere with our band (Wild Ram with Eddie Garrity) and they were the first ones to kind of make it from Wythenshawe. So we were quite jealous.

EDDIE GARRITY: There was no image in the audience that was at the second gig. But by then, nobody knew what punk was, so there was a mixture of hippies and just normally dressed people, you know and there'd be a few weird looking people so it was right across the board and I remember seeing a real mix of people there you know ... Because I'd been going to one gig and they'd all be dressed in your Slade gear or whatever, the Bowie kids and the Roxy kids, this was just totally, totally new, you know, bit of everything really.

MARK E. SMITH (lead singer: The Fall): There was a big split in the audience, that second time, between the punks – before it was punk, that is – and the glam rock lot. We were very anti-glam rock. To us it was sort of 'regular' ... Bowie covers ... just crap. You think these things are serious when you're a teenager, don't you?

WAYNE BARRETT: There was a message. The only message that we had at that time was getting the kids off the streets and having a good time. Watching a local band, basically, rather than going stealing cars.

MICK ROSSI: We got a little bit of press, which filtered back to London. We were really popular at the time in Wythenshawe and Manchester and our popularity was growing.

TONY WILSON: The reason why Slaughter and the Dogs do not seem to be punk was the glam element. They probably had a little bit too much Bowie and a little too much Mick Ronson, but nevertheless they were good. Let's get back to music, and tribute the late genius Mr Hannett (Martin Hannett, producer of Slaughter and the Dogs' first single, 'Cranked up Really High', who also produced Buzzcocks, Magazine, U2 and Joy Division: he died in 1991). 'Cranked up Really High' is one of the great punk records, it really is. 'Cranked Up Really High' is fantastic. When you get Jesus, you get quite a few John the Baptists; not the real thing, but leading to the real thing. Let's put them down as one of the John the Baptists.

IAN MOSS (audience member): Slaughter and the Dogs were a cabaret band, basically. They were kind of the back end of glam rock. They wanted to be rock stars.

MICK ROSSI: Manchester at the time, it was still the big bands that seemed to be so unreachable. It was so far away they were like living in Mars. Seeing the Sex Pistols sound check had a profound effect on me. We'd done our sound check and it was great, we were all happy. And then the Pistols had their sound check and Steve Jones sorted the chords of 'Anarchy' ... I thought, that sounds fucking good, (singing) 'De-de deh-deh.' John (Rotten) had a cold at the time and he got the lyrics out of his pocket on a horrible, dirty old snotty bit of paper.

Steve Jones 'pulling a furious guitar pose as a bemused longhair in velvet jacket looks into the distance' (Photo: Peter Oldham)

GLEN MATLOCK: I liked them (Slaughter and the Dogs) I thought they were a fun kind of band. I didn't really consider them to be a punk band, although they got involved in that 'cos that was what was going at the time. I became quite friendly with Rossi over the years. I found that he was really coming from more like the Spiders from Mars thing. Mick Ronson took him under his wing and he (was) heavily influenced by that period of the Bowie thing. Which was a cool place to come from, but everything became punk. Sometimes you have to jump on the coach, wherever its going. Whether it's going to where you want to go or not.

PETER HOOK: They were too cocky for me, Slaughter and the Dogs. I didn't like them. They were too arrogant; they were like these little wide boys. We used to share a practice place and Slaughter and the Dogs used to wait for all the bands to go home and they used to go and steal your gear. You'd come in and bleedin' Slaughter and the Dogs had done it again ...

IAIN GREY: Oh God, they were right tea leaves. They were from Wythenshawe.

Opinion on Slaughter on the Dogs still tends to divide people. But one thing was certain. The band were planning to give the July 20 show everything they'd got.

MICK ROSSI: We were thrilled. This is where Bowie played. This is where Lou Reed did 'White Heat'. This is where Ronson did *Slaughter on Tenth Avenue*. Just to be under the same roof as that ...

WAYNE BARRETT: ... all the good, great artists from the Seventies. So we were doing our mini concert of what they were doing basically. That's how I saw the gig.

Some of the people who attended the first decided to come back for more. They found a somewhat fuller Lesser Free Trade Hall than they'd witnessed six weeks earlier. The 'front parlour affair' as Morrisey had described it in his letter to the NME, was shaping up to be an altogether more aggressive affair.

PAUL MORLEY: I remember the first one being a sparse audience of people, very still and quite sober. I remember the second one being much more of a charge in the atmosphere and a much more exciting place to be. You got the sense that people like me, that had gone on their own the first time, definitely brought people back and said, 'You have got to see this, you will not believe this.'

PETER OLDHAM: Of course the great Malcolm McLaren was there as well. He took the money on the door.

PETE SHELLEY: He (McLaren) brought up a bus load of journalists to witness what was happening.

HOWARD DEVOTO: Certainly the Pistols bandwagon was going. By the time of the second gig, Malcolm had the clout. People were latching on to how hip it all was and he was able to get some of the journalists, music journalists, who were latching on to it: Caroline Coon (*Melody Maker*), Jonh Ingham (*Sounds*), certainly I remember them being there that night.

WAYNE BARRETT: Malcolm was some guy with red slippers in the Seventies, walking around with black leathers on and red slippers. It was like a Quentin Crisp kind of thing.

PETER HOOK: It was the second one that actually started the scene in Manchester, where everybody started getting involved with each other. The Drones and The Fall and everybody started mixing after the second one. The audience reaction at the first concert was quite quiet, they weren't going mad. By the time they got to the second one, that was when all the fighting started.

HOWARD DEVOTO: At that second gig, people were either getting what the Sex Pistols and ourselves were trying to achieve, or were prepared to give it a damn good go. There was the vibe, that there was something seriously happening now. Six weeks between the gigs, and the bandwagon had rolled on for them quite a lot, so it was feeling a bigger event all round.

PAUL MORLEY: There were like midgets dressed in bondage gear, which is the most *avant garde* thing you can ever imagine, because thirty years later that would still kind of scare you. This was very strange, out of some weird kind of science fiction film, the Sex Pistols entourage gathered at the front, kind of snooty about the strange Manchester people, because in a sense compared to what the Sex Pistols and their entourage looked like, we did have cloth caps and clogs on.

GARY AINSLEY (audience member): Well as far as I can remember, it sort of broke out in serious violence and there was a lot of chair smashing. I think the Sex Pistols had brought some groupies with them that weren't from Manchester.

GLEN MATLOCK: It was quite an eye opener to find that there was a scene somewhere other than the capital city. I know that sounds a bit kind of arrogant, but we just didn't know any better. The second gig was jumping, jumping. We premiered 'Anarchy in the UK', I think. Sorry, my chronological brain is a bit mixed up – for a variety of reasons.

PETER SHELLEY: I think that was the night they did 'Anarchy'. It was just like ... yeah, that's a single.

The Sex Pistols did indeed play their new song, 'Anarchy in the UK', for the very first time that night. They were live performance veterans by this stage. but for the first band due on stage before a packed hall, this was big stuff. The Buzzcocks' guitarist, Pete Shelley, had come prepared. The college kid had a cunning plan to upstage Slaughter and the Dogs. He'd bought a super-cheap guitar from Woolworths just prior to the gig – and he had no intention of the instrument surviving the Buzzcocks' set intact.

PETE SHELLEY: We didn't really have time to be nervous. I mean being nervous is a luxury when you've got time to think. I just remember Malcolm saying, 'If Buzzcocks aren't on in five minutes, they're not going on.' So we just had to get ready and on we go. The worst thing to do is to show the audience fear, because they can smell it. And when they know that you're nervous, that gets them nervous – and they don't like that. So if you can just go on and shout at them and play the music and get off, they think, wow, that's amazing. I was wearing ridiculously tight salmon pink jeans and a shirt which I had made myself; dark glasses, pumps ... and I just ended up smashing the guitar to pieces. Which was good fun and lots of noise. We didn't get lynched. It was really all about seeing what you could get away with. It's remarkable how much you can get away with before people say, 'Stop! Stop!' I'm still waiting for them to say stop.

HOWARD DEVOTO: People clapped. Did we do an encore? I doubt it. I should think we planned not to do an encore but to have our spectacular ending, where we all disappeared off separate bits of the stage and have a bit of a tussle with Peter's guitar. We were out there for twenty minutes and we got away with it and people clapped and we were in the music papers the following week.

PETE SHELLEY: Totally chaotic. I mean we all had a vague idea of what we were supposed to be doing so we had to make everything else up. I remember there being two long thin dressing rooms, but I mean we didn't have all that much dressing to do. We just went on and went off and packed up and ... got ready to watch the Sex Pistols. It was a case of just getting the gig and going, 'One, two, three, four!' and all finishing at the same time.

HOWARD DEVOTO: I seem to remember there being a Slaughter and the Dogs contingent there, because I certainly made a few disparaging remarks about them and there was some kind of hissing going on out there out in the auditorium.

MARK E. SMITH: I remember thinking, we could do better than that. The one thing they did do was break things down. The Free Trade Hall was ... not sacred, but it was like so *crap*. I'd been to a few shows there ... most of the groups that are coming back now – it's like a time warp for me.

PETE SHELLEY: Things like this didn't happen in Manchester, it was easy to contemplate spending a life of being completely unknown.

GLEN MATLOCK: The Buzzcocks played, I think it was their first gig. They had a guitar that was only half a guitar. He didn't like the top half and just cut it off with a tenant sword. I dug the way that when they finished their set – they finished up with 'Boredom' – there was an interminable guitar solo and Devoto just went up to Shelley and pulled his lead out. That was a good end to the set.

PETE SHELLEY: The whole basic premise of the band in the first place was so ridiculous and laughable, we were enjoying every moment of it, it was completely the wrong thing to do. We started doing the most uncommercial form of music you could possibly imagine and not even bothering to playing it very well. So as a result of that we didn't let our lack of experience stand in the way of having a go – it was perfect. Every day there was amazement over why we hadn't been arrested.

Up next are Slaughter and the Dogs. Wayne Barrett comes on stage in what can only be described as a backless, brown, silk blouse. Mick Rossi sports a red and white lady's shirt and a hairdo seemingly modelled on Dave Hill from Slade. They bang through their glam rock stompers and throw many shapes. A strange, curly-haired figure shakes a tambourine and dances on stage with them. Like an early version of Bez from the Happy Mondays. The atmosphere in the hall begins to darken.

HOWARD DEVOTO: If there was trouble, I don't really know about it. I know that the Lesser Free Trade Hall weren't prepared to take any more bookings afterwards. Whether that was down to something innocent like a bit of graffiti in the gents or something like that, I've no idea. But they certainly weren't anxious to accept any more bookings. I can't even think why.

PAUL MORLEY: The first band was Slaughter and the Dogs, who to me were a joke band at the time. One of my great claims to fame that no one knows, because it was all so early and ridiculous, is that I actually almost got thrown out of that second show. For some bizarre reason I was flinging peanuts at Wayne Barrett, the singer of Slaughter and the Dogs. I had no idea of what being punk was and I don't think it was even called punk then, but it seemed important for me to make a statement and my early statement, my first ever punk statement, was flinging peanuts at Wayne Barrett, because I thought he looked like a really dodgy copy of Bryan Ferry. He tried to get me thrown out. I didn't like Slaughter and the Dogs. But now, in hindsight, they are probably one of the great lost representatives of a true working class punk spirit. But it was exciting that there were Manchester bands.

PETE SHELLEY: I remember somebody losing a wallet and I went up and without the aid of any amplification shouted at everybody to be quiet. And announced a wallet had been found. It's all part of the public spiritedness.

PAUL MORLEY: I've never ever been a hooligan in my

life, I'd never been naughty at school and suddenly, faced with Wayne Barrett's hair, I just had to throw something at him to say, you are inauthentic. And I did.

PETER HOOK: A coachload of Cockneys came down and it started going off in a big fight between the Cockneys and the Mancs, for some unknown reason. It just got really heavy, the Buzzcocks set actually went okay, there was no trouble, but when the Sex Pistols came on, it all kicked off.

VANESSA CORLEY: It was rubbish. When the Pistols came on, half the audience started spitting and half the audience started retaliating. At the time I probably thought, what a waste of money – I'd rather be somewhere else.

LORRAINE JOYCE: It didn't last very long. They started throwing chairs and everything. I think that was the friends who they'd brought with them. It was just sort of set up.

EDDIE GARRITY: There was fights breaking out all the time. There was a big security team down there from Wythenshawe, maybe they started most of the fights. If it wasn't going to kick off, they'd probably been told to start trouble, with there being a lot of press down there, you know, get some publicity going.

PETER HOOK: It went off on the big fight and then Paul Morley was trying to get everybody going: 'Come on Mancs! Come on, let's get the Cockneys!' All running round. It was amazing.

PAUL MORLEY: I kind of got very over-excited. I was like a hyperactive little child.

PETER HOOK: I remember Mick Rossi was there. He's the little one out of Slaughter and the Dogs. He was like the one leading it all, leading the charges across the Lesser Free Trade Hall. Strange thing now is that I went back to a concert there and the room seemed so small. It's like going back to school and seeing your assembly. When you go back it's tiny.

PETER OLDHAM: The Buzzcocks and Slaughter and the Dogs were having a scrap at the side of the stage. It was like an Eric Morecambe thing, the curtain kept flicking and somebody kept dashing back on the other side.

EDDIE GARRITY: I was backstage, looking after the beer, so I was tucking into that. Then I thought I'd better go and look at this band, the Pistols. I went to the side of the stage and just stuck my head out and a bottle went 'ping', right on my head. I remember the Pistols came off and they were like pretty concerned, because all blood was running down my face. Johnny said to me, 'You want to go off to hospital with that.' I said, no ... just have another beer. All the lads were coming in, so I didn't want to seem soft. I'm there with blood pouring down my head, my mate Pete had been punched on the nose. Someone says, 'You're a right bloody mob, aren't you? Headbanger here and him with a nose bleed.' And the name sort of came about, that night (Ed Banger and the Nosebleeds).

There are two fascinating visual records of the gig. One is an eight millimetre cine film shot by a college friend of Devoto's called Mark Roberts. It features all three bands, but the majority of the time is given over to the Sex Pistols. Slaughter and the Dogs can be seen largeing around the stage. Pete Shelley is indeed wearing ridiculously tight

Steve Jones at the second Manchester gig: 'a Vivienne Westwood top
with zips on and a white Les Paul guitar' (Photo: Peter Oldham)

*salmon pink jeans. Johnny Rotten is sporting a silver belt
and a skinny black tie and at one point rips his shirt off.
Steve Jones is wearing a Vivienne Westwood top with zips
on and is using his trademark white Gibson Les Paul guitar,
with 1950's style pin-up girls stuck to it. Matlock is a vision
in pink. The audience's dress sense is a little snappier than
last time too.*

HOWARD DEVOTO: I think Mark shot three reels. We
decided, okay, we'll have one reel of us and then save two
for the Pistols. I don't even know if they knew they were
being filmed. Maybe we'd have said, 'Do you mind if we
film?' I've no idea actually.

PETER SHELLEY: It's like our copy of the Zupruder tapes (footage of the John F. Kennedy assassination) – instead of the grassy knoll, you can see Howard lurking onstage. It's like seeing Charlie Chaplin ... jerky pictures of yourself.

HOWARD DEVOTO: It's curious, because for a start, there's no sound. It's like seeing silent movie footage or something, but I think for somebody who hadn't handled a movie camera before, Mark actually did a very good job with it.

The second record is a set of still photographs taken by student Peter Oldham. The black and white pictures of all three groups are reproduced in this book. My favourite is of Steve Jones, pulling a furious guitar pose as a rather bemused longhair in a velvet jacket looks into the distance to locate the bar. Oldham had also been to the first gig and afterwards had made a note that if the band returned, he'd 'take a few snaps'.

PETER OLDHAM: I thought, I'll get some pictures of that, more for my own amusement than anything. For one thing you weren't going to take your best camera down there just in case somebody ripped it out of your hands or it got confiscated, so it was a matter of just popping up out of your seat with your Zenith and flashing a few pictures. I'm a much better photographer now. I'm glad I took the photographs in as much as they're a record of the event more than anything.

Because it's all 'kicking off' in the hall, the Sex Pistols set is shorter than last time. The time had come for the most important part of the evening. Counting the cash.

HOWARD DEVOTO: Malcolm had his hand fairly firmly on the tiller of the money boat. We weren't doing it for the money. We were doing it just to play our gigs. Maybe we got slipped ten quid for getting to the end of our set.

PETE SHELLEY: All the proceeds went to Malcolm. We got £10 as our fee. I don't know what happened to the rest of the money. He spent it on the Sex Pistols. You could live like a king for £10. More than a whole week's dole money.

MICK ROSSI: They were upstairs, counting the money. Malcolm's going, one for you, one for me ...

WAYNE BARRETT: ... one up the trouser leg and all the rest of it. I think he must have screwed us for round about a hundred and fifty quid, something like that.

MICK ROSSI: Allegedly.

WAYNE BARRETT: Allegedly.

PETER OLDHAM: I nearly ran them over on Oxford Road, the Sex Pistols, on the way to the second gig. They were going across for a burger or something on Oxford Road. Could have changed musical history really, couldn't I?

MICK ROSSI: The aim after the Free Trade Hall thing was then for us to try and hit London and we had a few false starts but we finally got there. That was the next step. Then records. Because we started to realise then what was going on.

WAYNE: Malcolm suggested to go down and to try and play in the Roxy, and centre around that area, so when we

A seminal rock moment: Sex Pistols onstage at the Lesser Free Trade Hall, July 20, 1976 (Photo: Peter Oldham)

went down to London, that's when we did tidy our look up before going down there.

MICK: No more irons basically.

WAYNE: No more irons, no more satin and things like that. The brown thing I was wearing at the Free Trade Hall, I think it was my mum who made that.

PAUL MORLEY: I saw the Sex Pistols a dozen times and for me it was the equivalent of seeing Elvis Presley 'cos it was always fantastic. It was always the most remarkable kind of show. It was like extreme show business. It was real show business ... they were entertainers, they weren't sloppy or anything, they put their heart and soul into it and they really worked hard. At that second show, you just got the feeling that something really important had happened.

The confusion in people's minds over the two Sex Pistols gigs at the Lesser Free Trade Hall will probably never be fully separated. Too much time and too many mind-altering liquids and substances have passed through many of those at the gigs by now. It is probably true to say that although nowhere near as good on the evidence of those present – it was more of an event – the concert on 20 July 1976 probably did more than anything to create the shape of the music scene in Manchester over the twenty-five years. More people were physically there to spread the word, to form bands, to start writing for the music press and to get their flared trousers taken in sharpish. The next step was to get the Six Pistols on the TV and into people's homes. Then it could all really kick off.

5: Even Better Than the Lovely Joni Mitchell

IN WHICH MR WILSON INTRODUCES THE TELEVISION
VIEWER TO THE SEX PISTOLS FOR THE VERY FIRST TIME.

THE SEX PISTOLS' appearance on local television on December 1, 1976, sealed their national notoriety. The 'filth and the fury' that was broadcast on Thames Television's Today *programme consisted of Rotten saying 'shit' twice – very quietly – and guitarist Steve Jones calling host Bill Grundy a 'dirty bastard', a 'dirty fucker' and a 'fucking rotter.' This was, quite possibly, the last ever use of the word 'rotter' on mainland Britain. Very few people even saw the item, as the* Today *show was only broadcast in the London area. Because it made the front pages of the tabloid press the following day, many people assume this was the Pistols' first television appearance. It wasn't. The first time the Sex Pistols appeared on British television was on* So It Goes, *recorded at Granada Television in Manchester three months earlier. The programme was presented by Tony Wilson, abetted by cultural 'commentator' Clive James and, occasionally, by satirist Peter Cook. It was a very odd programme indeed. But events leading up to the show were even stranger:* Carry On Swastika, *if you will. It's amazing it was ever broadcast, but broadcast it was – albeit in a slightly doctored form.*

TONY WILSON (presenter: *So It Goes***):** In late '75, early '76, my friends and I here at Granada were preparing to turn our regional *What's On* programme into a late night music show. And, we were turning it into a comedy show, with Clive James doing comedy sketches. We were doing a comedy show because there was, in our opinion, no music worth covering.

CHRIS PYE (producer: *So It Goes***):** It was a proper TV show, you understand. It was just because of the people we were dealing with … it got a little bit sort of edgy sometimes. But it was a normal schedule; we had a studio and cameramen, the sound guys turned up and the floor manager wore the headphones. It was all quite normal. Until the Sex Pistols turned up.

PETER WALKER (director: *So It Goes***):** I worked for Granada for twenty-one years. I started out on sound and then eventually became a dubbing mixer and then a director but I had a hankering to do music. I became involved in lots of kids' shows, *The Arrows, The Bay City Rollers* and eventually a programme called *So It Goes*. I was the automatic choice to be the director because there was nobody else around at the time to do that sort of show. Chris Pye – and myself to a lesser extent – didn't really didn't want them (the Sex Pistols) on the programme. They'd been in Tony Wilson's mind right from the word go. Every pre-production meeting we'd have about who was going to be on that week's show, he would say, 'When are we going to get the Sex Pistols on?' Oh Tony, belt up, you can't have them on, they're not musical,

'It caught on an undertone, a feeling within the country': The Pistols launch into 'Anarchy in the UK' on *So It Goes* (Photo: Granada TV)

they're not musicians, they're just layabouts. I think Chris finally relented under pressure and said, 'Okay ... they're on the last show.'

TONY WILSON: It was the last show of the first series that one was able to infiltrate ... it was really a question of getting the Pistols on the last show. The entire British press – with the exception of *The Times* and the *Daily Mail* – hated *So It Goes,* they hated it. And I mean *hated* it. In fact, we were responsible for a great resurgence of love for *The Old Grey Whistle Test*, because these disgraceful people on *So It Goes* were not treating music with the respect it deserved.

PETER WALKER: Before the Sex Pistols turned up, the

programme was very much Chris Pye's baby. He was the instigator behind the whole series. He was very much influenced by bands like The Eagles and the East Coast, cool, laid-back, American sound, and absolutely besotted by Eric Clapton. He (Pye) was a bit of a guitarist himself. He just couldn't understand why he should put on a band who couldn't really play that well and were more into three or four chords at the most.

CHRIS PYE: We had Clive James on every show doing a monologue. We had a guy called Steve who came on and reviewed films he'd never seen. We said to him, 'What do you make of this week's movie?' He'd never seen the movie, but he talked fluently for about a minute and a half. It wasn't a magazine show, it was like a kind of bits and pieces show.

PETER WALKER: The show for Tony was a different proposition. He wanted to have a lot of exposure. He was very much an egocentric sort of presenter, very much involved in what the programme looked like, how he wanted it to be. And the music, perhaps at that stage, was secondary to his own career

PAUL MORLEY: Tony Wilson had a weird energy and a fantastic ability to persuade the powers-that-be. It was ridiculous to be able to get a music show on television. Unbelievable. But that's what was fantastic about it. Tony Wilson in the North West in '76, '77, '78 was like John Stapleton *(GMTV)* or Richard Madeley *(This Morning)*. It kind of looked like that. Tony, as much as he was on it very quickly, was always one step behind. He still had the long hair and the flares and the leather blouson jacket. Clearly an interesting show that put on the best new music, but it was presented by the most peculiar character and got lacerating reviews from London. They couldn't understand why suddenly this very square-looking bloke was presenting this hip show. Also, what was fascinating about it was that Tony Wilson's sidekick was Clive James, who presented this kind of weird little essay on pop culture.

TONY WILSON: We'd enjoy making jokes. We'd have Clive James being Demis Roussos, or we'd have Peter Cook talking about his obscene album of that period. So we did a comedy show, with these rather ordinary bands. The pub rock bands, I wouldn't have anything to do with. But then again, they wouldn't have anything to do with a late night TV show. It was just an awful period. All that crap on *Top of The Pops*. As I point out to people, then, just like it is today, it loooked exactly the same. People were exactly as badly dressed. There were one or two good pop songs, mostly it was dribble. Very similar to today.

All television programmes are, by their very nature and structure, stressful creatures. But So It Goes seems to have been specially designed to be as difficult to make as possible.

CHRIS PYE: The whole thing was a bit fraught. You had to wait for Clive James to arrive, because he came by train. Some shows we had Peter Cook on, but we had to send somebody down to London to get him; we didn't want him to drink too much on the train. So that was all a bit dodgy.

PETER WALKER: The one big difference on that particular day was the Sex Pistols. Now we'd obviously heard about their career so far and we knew that they were not dangerous, shall we say, but unorthodox in the way that they presented themselves and the way they performed.

JORDAN (punk muse): The combination of Peter Cook, Clive James and the Sex Pistols and all those weird, hippie bands, and Tony and that denim and clogs ... well, it's got to be a winner.

Indeed a winner it was. What makes the Sex Pistols' performance on So It Goes even more remarkable is to see it in the context of the whole programme; with the comedy and with the performances of the other groups. They only get three minutes air-time at the end of a half-hour show, but they stand out like the sorest of thumbs. And the way the performance is altered in the end actually increases its power.

TONY WILSON: I don't think that I was that arrogant at that time to refuse to have bands in the studio. I wouldn't consider the Rick Wakemans and pub rock and shit. I wasn't that arrogant but nevertheless I wouldn't have wanted to even bother with any of that shite. It was awful, awful. That was the last show of the series ... couldn't get any fucking bands at all. We decided that we'd have three unsigned bands, the Pistols being one of them. But the other ones, they were all crap.

JORDAN: Tony couldn't have been nicer. He was really, really charming and nice to the band and really calm about it. I would imagine he probably didn't know what was going to happen till it did happen. It was a very 'by the seat of your pants' sort of performance. Not even John would know what was going to happen till he did it.

PETER WALKER: Nobody, apart from perhaps Tony, had seen them (the Pistols) performing live. I think there was a lot of angst in the studios about what they were going to do: are they going to start smashing up the place? Are they going to be like The Who? The Who, once a upon a time, came in and they just destroyed the studio.

JORDAN: I think John (Johnny Rotten) was a bit nervy about it on the way up, because I remember the train journey. It was a bit of a worry, but once he got there, once he saw Tony Wilson with his jeans jacket and his clogs, we knew we'd made it. We just called him a bloody hippie when we walked in: 'My God! What do you think you look like, bloody hippie?' We didn't know what to expect – music companies were all full of hippies – but we didn't really expect Tony to be a hippie. We gave him such a hard time. I'm so sorry Tony, in retrospect.

To watch So It Goes *today is something of a challenge. The title sequence is a series of shape-changing caterpillars and snails that evolve into a droog-like image of Tony Wilson, as if taken from* A Clockwork Orange. *Then Jordan pops up and declares, to camera, that: 'The Sex Pistols are, if possible, even better than the lovely Joni Mitchell.' So far, so baffled.*

JORDAN: Tony Wilson asked me to get up and introduce the band and he said, you can say whatever I wanted really. I think he thought I was just going to say, 'Here's the Sex Pistols.' But I didn't. I think it was something to do with the Bowles Brothers (who were also on the show) There was an argument – involving John – and Joni Mitchell was mentioned. John made it up to get up their noses.

After Jordan's introduction, the music commences. The first band up play superbly, but these boys are in the wrong place at the wrong time. Over the next thirty minutes, the shape of rock changes right under the platform-soled feet of the group known as Gentlemen. They are pomp-rockers from North Manchester. They whack out 'My Ego's Hurting Me'. They are super-complex and confident. They rhyme 'what a drag you are' with 'Jaguar' and at one point, the bass player and lead guitarist swap left hands and fret each other's instruments. One of their number sports flared and fringed leather trousers. After five minutes of gesticulating, they finish. 'Nice one!' declares Wilson.

CHRIS PYE (TV producer): Bloody hell, who are Gentlemen?

PETER WALKER (director): I remember nothing about Gentlemen obviously, because who would have a crap name like Gentlemen? Don't know why we ever had them on. Gentlemen? Come on, do me a favour.

GLEN MATLOCK: Didn't realise there were any other bands on with us.

HOWARD DEVOTO: Wow, there were other bands? I would doubt that we would have sat through any other bands that were on, that would have been all part of the attitude.

The next band up are the Bowles Brothers. They lay down 'Charlie's Nuts', an acoustic, summery jazz number, with plenty of 'skoodly-doodly-wah-wah's' thrown in.

JORDAN: It was truly bizarre – not just the other bands, but the audience. They were just like … they looked like prisoners waiting to die. They were just gone. They'd had it, brain dead, whole lot of them, hadn't got a clue. But then, if you look at the previous bands that were on the show, you can see why they'd been lulled into this sort of catatonic state. Diddlie diddlies and blinkin' split jeans and flared leather jackets. It was a madhouse. We were sitting in this dressing room, listening to this folk band with a double bass. We didn't know what we had let ourselves in for.

Next, under the heading of 'Brain Damage', Clive James does a monologue directly to camera about music press apathy.

HOWARD DEVOTO: Malcolm did invite Pete and I down to the *So It Goes* thingy. I guess they wanted as much support as they could. I've got very confused memories of that day. I seem to remember Clive James being on. There was an audience and Clive James was trying to kind of get this rapport going. Meanwhile, the Pistols were trying to sort of psyche themselves up to perform. There was definitely a fair bit of antagonism going on between the band and Clive James

GLEN MATLOCK: Clive James was on the show and he thought, well, I'm going to take Rotten on. And Rotten just made mincemeat of him. Absolute mincemeat.

TONY WILSON: I remember the Pistols were extremely badly behaved all day. I remember them lying on the floor of the reception foyer here at Granada, which was quite funny and upset people. I remember Malcolm giving me a tee-shirt – which I still have – of a teenage boy smoking. I remember Clive James in the green room getting very upset with them and having an argument with them and not liking them. That was the day, that moment, that Clive James grew old. Cause Clive didn't get it. He still doesn't. He and Lydon (Johnny Rotten) had a real row and he hated that. It was all a bit chaotic.

JORDAN: Peter Cook was on, he was really cool, he was really great. He was sort of a bit drunk and a bit nervy. He thought the band were great, he really liked them. He threw me a packet of fags across the studio. And there was this bloke, Clive James. I think his life changed after that day, I think he was never the same man again. He was upset, he thought the band were in bad taste. John and I laid into him really badly and called him a baldie old Sheila at the top of our voices ... 'You baldie old Sheila!'

The only warning of things to come is a cleverly played-in clip of Jerry Lee Lewis, performing up-close and dirty to a bunch of Sixties kids at Granada TV studios. It's a performance that's worth a book in itself. Lewis, his sweat-bathed face covered by a hanging, curled fringe, is genuinely terrifying. His appearance is actually upsetting; it's an horrific and terrific piece of television. Coming out of the clip, Wilson points to it as containing 'energy so lacking in today's big bands. Perhaps coke isn't the real thing.'

Clive James then interviews Peter Cook about the Derek and Clive Live album. The satirist's hands are visibly shaking and he refers to Dudley Moore as a 'midget poof'. Cook gets a few laughs from the audience. He would have another involvement with punk, at its tail end. In 1978 Cook presented ATV's Revolver show. In this late night shout-fest, he played the part of a reluctant club host, introducing punk/new wave bands of the day. After they had played, he would invariably insult them, before bringing on the next group. Then the process would repeat itself. It was so punk rock.

PETER WALKER: All the rehearsals went fine. Then they went, oh, they're nice enough, they're just, you know, a group of lads, pleasant. But when it came to transmission and they started to perform, that was just a total eye opener. Nobody could believe it. There was so much energy coming out of that group, so much commitment. They saved that performance for when they knew the cameras were rolling.

JORDAN: I think the Pistols did quite a tame rehearsal in the afternoon, I'm not even sure if it was the same song, I think they sang something else. So it wasn't anything like the final product. The crew were led to believe it was going to be peachy and nice, but I mean they would have been stupid to think that. The thing about the Pistols is they did, to some extent, feed off other people's aggression. When the crowds just got so adoring, when the audience got so adoring, the Pistols weren't quite themselves any more. You can see it in that shot of John at the end; he was feeding off the negativity that was coming from the crowd. In a way he didn't really like people liking him because it meant that he wasn't doing it right.

GLEN MATLOCK: We were big 'eads! It was good that we got a break on the TV so more people could see us. I've always said the way we got it together, it's got a direct analogy with the *Blues Brothers* movie. They were going round, getting everybody out of jail, 'Hey, we've got to get a band together! We're on a mission from God!' We were like, on a mission to stir things up a little bit and get something happening. So getting a TV show was one more step up the ladder. We considered it our right ... 'cos we were those kind of guys.

CHRIS PYE: Before the Pistols came along we tended to take bands that were not Top Twenty bands. Tony led the music policy really, so we didn't very often have straight up and down bands. We had people who were just slightly off kilter. That's what the policy was. We booked the Pistols – we knew they were kind of out there somewhere – so we booked them. And they went off the scale. I knew nothing about them at all until they arrived, they were difficult, they were odd, they were not what you expect. But they were a great booking.

GLEN MATLOCK: I haven't seen it (*So It Goes*) for a long time. You always see the little clip, and you don't see the whole show.

CHRIS PYE: During the afternoon, we were rehearsing the band and eventually we got a phone call from the sixth floor, which was the management floor. In Granada, you can view what's going on in all the studios by turning your TV set on, an internal service. Sydney Bernstein was chairman of the company. He'd been skimming through the channels and came across the Sex Pistols in the studio rehearsing. One of the Sex Pistols entourage (Jordan) was wearing a swastika armband. Sydney, for a man of his age and his generation and his background, was really, really upset by this. He thought it was absolutely outrageous that we should be transmitting somebody with a swastika armband on a Granada programme. He wasn't worried about their hair. He wasn't worried about the fact they were aggressive. He thought the swastika was really in bad taste. So he called down to me and said, 'This can't go out.' So it was my task to try to persuade the Sex Pistols that this was a jolly good idea to take off the swastika armband. The issue occupied about three hours.

JORDAN: Somebody noticed that I was wearing a shirt with a swastika armband and there was a real big do about it. I got taken in secrecy through this labyrinth of sets and corridors into wardrobe. There was a lot of gnashing of teeth and sucking of lips. And me sort of standing my ground really. I said, 'That's the shirt, that's the way it should be, it's sewn on, I'm not taking it off, I'm not taking the shirt off.' Everyone got involved and there was a big do over it.

PETER WALKER: She (Jordan) came to rehearsals wearing a German-style uniform with a big swastika armband. Our head of Granada TV at the time was Sydney Bernstein, who didn't actually like the Germans. We weren't allowed to have German microphones on the station. I was under very strict instructions not to show her or her armband in shot. But of course the Sex Pistols were very adamant that she had to be there, because she was part of their act.

JORDAN: I didn't know what had caused it, I just knew somebody must have spotted it. Firstly, I didn't think anything of it. Secondly, I thought if somebody did notice it, I'd get away with it. I really was a bit bemused by it all.

CHRIS PYE: I met Malcolm McLaren, because we had to talk to him about a couple of problems we had between the rehearsal and the show. I didn't know how to handle these guys, I didn't know how best to talk to them. So Malcolm was around and he was the intermediary between the TV studio and people like me and the band.

The Pistols in the Granada TV studio with Jordan stageside, her swastika armband covered up (Photo: Granada TV)

TONY WILSON: It's hard to remember the Nazi chic of punk. In the early days of the Pistols, anything Nazi was a way of shock, outrage, or whatever. On that particular afternoon, Jordan had a swastika armband on. I had to go and tell her, 'Listen, sorry love ...' So if you look at the video she has gaffer tape over the swastika armband. It was a wild day and unruly. They caused lots of trouble. Thank God.

CHRIS PYE: I think Tony spoke to the band because Tony was that kind of guy. Tony, he'll speak to anybody. I was more involved with trying to keep things calm. I was on 'keeping things calm' mode that day. I think Tony thought the band were great. I think he loved them. I've no idea what they made of him. They had a bit of a falling out. I think that they thought that Tony was some kind of ageing, naff person, because he was a TV presenter and he had really quite nice hair. I think they thought he was perhaps, from a different generation.

TONY WILSON: I was a hippie, I was! I mean, if you look at me on *So It Goes*, introducing the Sex Pistols ...

CHRIS PYE: I worked out that if I went to talk to them – I was an even naffer person than Tony Wilson – they wouldn't be responding to me. So I said to Malcolm, this is not something that I think is the right thing. It will offend people and it's a big audience. I know you want to be an offensive band, an aggressive band, but it would be really helpful if you could take the armband off.

I just said to him, 'It would be really, really helpful Malcolm, really, really helpful, if you get that armband off.' And he went away into some room where they were and eventually, when it went on the air, the armband had not come off, but the swastika itself had been covered up. A sufficient compromise.

JORDAN: Some bright spark came up with the idea that they would stick a piece of white tape over it – which I didn't want, Malcolm didn't want. There was another argument and in the end it came down to either you don't go on the show or you have it censored. Which it was. It looks kind of good being censored, because people think it's even more powerful, probably because they tried to stop me showing it. Some years later, after that incident with Clive, he wrote an article in the *Observer* and he was still banging on about it. He was really so seriously affronted and yet, it was just commonplace to us. He was being a twit, he's so straight. He was on a TV programme and he brought it up again, he brought up the incident with me and the shirt again 'cause it offended him so badly.

GLEN MATLOCK: They wanted us to do one number and we wanted to do two. And originally Tony Wilson had just wanted to interview John (Rotten). John didn't really want to. I think he was a bit cagey about it. We didn't want him to do that, 'cause it was like, Ooh, he's getting more attention than us! They compromised and said well, you can do two, but we'll only record one.

It was on a Sunday night and it was running really late and the cameramen were going to get triple time or whatever it was, if it went over the witching hour. I broke a string in the first number and didn't have a spare guitar. So somebody had to go all the way to the dressing rooms that were on the other side of the studio, bring the string back and I laboriously put it on. Tony Wilson was trying to chat Rotten up. You know, 'Why wouldn't you come and talk to me? Are you afraid to talk to us?' I just piped up, 'No, it's because you're a cunt.' All the audience laughed.

TONY WILSON: If Glen was rude to me, that's a bit of a surprise, because Glen was the nice one. Great musicians are meant to be rude to tossers from the media. No problem with that.

CHRIS PYE: We rehearsed with them and they were not like anything I'd ever seen before. They were loud and brash and violent and, in my view, unmusical. And completely unco-operative. They were just weird. I'd never seen people like this before. They were just a ... thing. A fully-formed live force. And it was difficult.

JORDAN: Soon as they (the audience) saw the Pistols come on – if you look at the footage of it – John's just like staring at them, daring 'em, you know? Drop dead! (laughing). And they didn't move ... the whole gig! ... they didn't move at all. Just stood there ... just sat there.

Wilson delivers a link to camera, referring back to the Clive James/Peter Cook chat, stating that the Derek and Clive album has a warning on it. 'Our final live band tonight also have a warning on them. One of the most reviewed and reviled phenomenon of recent weeks ... Sex Pistols.'

TONY WILSON: Either Matlock or Jones hits the guitar and you get this noise. I'm looking like this dumb ex-hippie – which of course I am – a dumb ex-hippie in my denims. And you get the noise. Then you get I think Lydon (Rotten) screams, 'Woodstock ... coming to get yer!' Then they hit it. And it was stunning.

Rotten advises the audience to 'Get off your arse!' and the band, dressed in a mish-mash of Kings Road clobber, home-made gear and brothel creepers, play 'Anarchy in the UK', the song they'd played live for the first time at the Lesser Free Trade Hall on 20 July. Whatever your opinion of the Sex Pistols, it is an extraordinary performance.

PETER WALKER: Because it was the first TV they'd ever done, they were just giving everything they could possibly give it to make their point. Watching the pictures on the monitors was just amazing. The energy was reflected back from them, to me and back to them again. It was something new. It was totally different but it wasn't a breath of fresh air at all. You had underlying foulness in the air, if you like. It caught on to an undertone, a feeling within the country.

PETE SHELLEY: The *So It Goes* broadcast at Granada ... both me and Howard went down. On one copy of the film, you actually see me and Howard on the opening shot. On another copy, you don't see us at all. We've been edited out of history.

PAUL MORLEY: You can see their entourage. You can see Shelley and Devoto in the audience and get a little hint of what it was like before the hype and the tabloid nonsense got hold of it: as an artistic kind of liberation. It was those early months that were important and it was great that *So It Goes* was around to trap it, to capture it.

HOWARD DEVOTO: I don't think we saw the whole programme. We probably hung out a bit with them (Sex Pistols) and turned up. We were there for their slot. I remember them being very effective. I also remember Jordan's not entirely successful attempts to try and get a bit of trouble going down at the front of the stage by knocking a plastic chair over. But yeah, they were great on it.

JORDAN: I actually really wanted to just throw the chair at the audience, but it's not on really. They wouldn't have noticed if they got hit in the face anyway. It nearly hit Steve (Jones) I think and he had to kick it out of the way. I was doing what we'd normally do at a gig really. It was a very strange setting.

PETER HOOK: There's very few experiences you remember in your life that aren't sexual and I remember watching TV and I was just sat at home having my tea, Friday evening I think it was, the Sex Pistols were on Granada.

Oh my God, 'Anarchy in the UK', when he threw a chair at Jordan. It was fantastic,

JORDAN: I think it was a great success I think they thought it was, but they were very disappointed about the audience and the atmosphere. But if you look at it, that's what makes it such a great performance.

The broadcast version of 'Anarchy in the UK' ends in a phase-out cacophony. Glen Matlock kicks over a mike stand and Jordan does the Twist on the stage. The last shot is of Rotten, staring at the cameramen for what seems to be an age, underscored by a few seconds of feedback. It looks as if the tape has been tampered with. That's because it had been tampered with.

PETER WALKER: The original? That was edited slightly at the end. The end of the number was totally different to what you see now. They started to kick the microphone stand around, kick the drums apart, kick the amplifiers over. They were doing a big job on their own kit on the stage. The young lady who was at the side with the armband on joined in. And I was under strict instructions not to show her at all on the television. The whole thing ended with all the chaos and all the gear falling apart with him just staring into the lens. Really, really long, long stare. The audience were just totally silent. They didn't know whether to applaud or not. That look saved it, because what I could do then was go back and edit that look into the previous section, so it looked like the song was coming to an end. When in actual fact it never did.

JORDAN: The song overran, John wasn't ready to stop. He was giving quite a lot of verbal to the audience and knocking the stuff around. But he wasn't smashing the studio up. The equipment was getting knocked around a bit and he was getting really annoyed.

TONY WILSON: The studio audience of two hundred even dumber hippies, sitting there for a music show, are also utterly flabbergasted. They'd rehearsed three and a quarter minutes of this new song, but of course they just went on and they went on and on and on. They did seven minutes and the last two minutes they were kicking the set apart. As they hit the last chord, I'm sitting there with a large grin on my face. The wonderful thing is, when the last note hits ... and stops ... there is complete silence. Two hundred people ... nothing ... just silence. Suddenly, you hear Chris Pye. He's running down from the control box and he's coming down the stairs to hit one of them for going three minutes over and kicking his set apart. They actually jump off stage and they run out the door. So by the time the producer arrives and says, 'Where the hell are they!' they've gone, they've escaped. It was great.

PETER WALKER: That would be very typical of Chris Pye, to run down the stairs. He's a company man, he always was a company man. He knew that would reflect on his standing within Granada.

CHRIS PYE: I think I may have gone for a bit of a lie down at that stage. I felt really relieved it had finished and it was all over. I thought we had put something on the air that was so different and so extraordinary and that most people would find it difficult and offensive and rude. I knew there'd be people complaining. You just knew the phones would be ringing when the show went out.

After the performance, Wilson states: 'Bakunin would have loved it, that was Sex Pistols, the leaders in their field.' Mikhail Bakunin was a leading 19th century anarchist.

TONY WILSON: Why would Bakunin have loved it? Who said that? Did I say that?

I can't believe I said that — did I say that? Oh God … well, the idea that I am a posing bloody idiot is very correct. It's 'cos I loved it. I was always very proud they were on. It's good art. Bakunin *would* have loved it. Without a doubt. Great art. Groundbreaking, revolutionary, breaking down barriers. And shocking and upsetting and a great tune. A great tune and great art.

The end title music of So It Goes *is 'Drift Away' … as in … 'I wanna get lost in your rock and roll and drift away.' A caption appears proposing that 'One day, we'll look back on this and it will all seem funny … ' The quote is attributed to Bruce Springsteen, 1973.*

TONY WILSON: One of the things I liked most, looking back at that tape, is the line I say: 'One of the most reviled phenomenon of recent weeks' – and we're the other one, because everyone hated us – and that's just the phrase of recent weeks. That's how absolutely current this moment was.

CHRIS PYE: I wasn't scared about the reaction, I just knew there'd *be* a reaction. I wasn't scared about it, because we set the show up to do things that other people wouldn't do. Therefore, the fact that people were going to call in and complain was actually quite good news. At the end of the show there was a sense of real elation. It wasn't just the elation that we'd managed to finish the show, it was elation that we put something on the air that was really, really extraordinary. Really, a wild moment of excitement. I was the wrong generation. Maybe if I'd been fifteen years younger. I didn't really realise at that stage how punk rock was going to become the enormous style movement that it was. It wasn't clear then, so I didn't know that this was a moment which was going to define music television.

PETER WALKER: At the time I didn't realise it was going to be a historical document. One of the reasons it became a historical document, I think a young chap called Julian Temple grabbed hold of it and used it in various films – his *Rock 'n' Roll Swindle* and other feature films he made after that. If that hadn't happened I don't think it would have become that much of a piece of footage.

CHRIS PYE: The bosses said to me, 'Who are they, what was that all about, they were bloody awful!' We had that kind of reaction. But nobody said to me, you should never have done that, or, you made a mistake. Everyone just said, 'Bloody hell, what was that?'

PETER WALKER: After the performance, we invited everybody over to the green room to have a drink. We thought we'd better lock up the spirits and the heavy liquor, 'cos these guys are going to be trouble. After the programme, the Sex Pistols were in the corridor outside the room on the floor, sitting, just having a drink. We're all saying, 'Come on and join us'. They said, 'Oh no, we're alright here. Honest, we don't want to be any trouble.'

They just quietly sat there drinking, never bothered a soul and afterwards said, 'Goodnight, thanks very much for the programme, hope to see you again Mr Walker.' Very nice.

JORDAN: I think that show in particular really stands the test of time, that part with the Sex Pistols in it. I think drawing the comparison between the bands that were on the show and the Pistols is just an amazing thing. It really does highlight just how far ahead of their time the Sex Pistols were and how it still lingers today in some forms. That show was really ground breaking. There was, to my knowledge, nothing going on in London with Thames TV or any of the stations there at that time that could match it. There really wasn't in my mind anything quite as good as that in London. So some transition had happened, be it to do with the Sex Pistols or that show ... or just the attitude of the people who live up here.

TONY WILSON: I'm proud of the seventy-eight bands me and my colleagues put on television (for the series of *So It Goes*). But I'm really proud of bands we didn't – because we were right about them as well.

ALAN HEMSPALL: Three or four months later, Bill Grundy's TV show occurred. A few choice effing and jeffing moments on his show and suddenly they were news.

JORDAN: John (Rotten) was quite an introverted person, not the sort of guy who'd like to go out clubbing. He was quite a quiet, thinking person, quite unlike Steve who was a bit of a lad. I think that comes through very obviously when they're on stage; they've all got their own little character to play.

'The last shot is of Rotten, staring at the cameramen for what seems to be an age': Johnny Rotten on *So It Goes* (Photo: Granada TV)

PETER WALKER: I met Johnny Rotten years later and he was just the same. He was still a nice bloke. That's the thing that when you look at the footage … he is a nice bloke and then something takes hold of him. A demon takes hold of him.

6: They All Spat at Him

IN WHICH THE AUDIENCE MAKES GOOD (MUSIC) AND
THERE IS MUCH TALK OF 'POST PUNK'.

ON OCTOBER 8, 1976, the Sex Pistols signed a £40,000
contract with EMI. The relationship wasn't going to last
long – they would end up at Virgin via A&M – but from
that point onward, the Sex Pistols were part of the music
industry. That industry, and more importantly the way we
access it, was about to change, thanks to the next move
planned by the Buzzcocks. Six months after their first real
gig, the entrepreneurial Buzzcocks became the first punk
band to set-up their own record label. In January 1977,
they released the Spiral Scratch EP on the New Hormones
label. It was £1 a pop. The distance between the band and
the audience had just become even shorter.

HOWARD DEVOTO: The idea of doing our own record
label, New Hormones, I wouldn't say that came from the
Pistols in any sense. They'd signed to EMI by the time we
were getting *Spiral Scratch* together. By then, Stiff Records
had started. I did have a word with Dave Robinson (head of
Stiff Records) when we were trying to pull that together, to
see whether he had any helpful advice. I don't recall him

having any helpful advice whatsoever – he was kind of vaguely encouraging. I think that the second gig was perhaps particularly impactful. Because what people saw that night, they didn't only see the Sex Pistols, they saw Buzzcocks, who were a local group. I think that actually had a big impact on people. It was a big deal to borrow money from your friends and to go through the whole thing and go to a vaguely proper recording studio and have records made and then give them to shops and start talking wholesale price. I remember Malcolm (McLaren) saying to me when he first saw *Spiral Scratch* in Rough Trade or Bizarre Records, the handful of shops that were stocking it, he was saying, it's quite odd seeing this record that has come from nowhere.

PETE SHELLEY: Our agent wanted to become a record producer, so he called himself Martin Zero instead of Martin Hannett. We believed him that he was a record producer – we were just as gullible as everybody else. Instead of going to the record company cap in hand, or trying to get an A&R guy to come up to Manchester, you decided you didn't need that and you just did it yourself. He (Hannett) suggested making a record. He thought he could get some studio time, some down-time at a studio. So because of that it wasn't going to cost us anything. But all that fell through, so then we started researching. Well, how would you go and make a record? We found we could get 1,000 copies done for 500 quid.

HOWARD DEVOTO: We had to learn it ourselves, piece it together: where could you get records pressed, how do you go about doing it, have we really got to settle for those injection-moulded ones where you didn't get a proper stick-on label? They were the only ones that would press a small run of 1,000 singles or maybe they were a little bit cheaper or something because there wasn't a stick-on label. Maybe it was Martin Hannett. I think he may have had some contact, because he was really pretty new to it as well.

PETE SHELLEY: I might have still been sat in Leigh, playing in my bedroom thinking, Ooh, if only I can get a record company to listen to my music. It's almost like the Gordian Knot, which Alexander had so intricately tied and nobody could undo it. He just got his knife and sliced it in two and solved the problem. By exercising your will you can make things happen. So everything which has happened since is a direct result of that.

The EP was funded by money begged and borrowed from friends and family by Devoto and Richard Boon, a former schoolfriend who had now become the Buzzcocks' manager. From office space housed with the now-defunct listings magazine New Manchester Review, *they worked out they needed to sell 600 copies to break even. Ambitiously, the EP had a picture cover, with the band snapped by polaroid in Manchester's Piccadilly Gardens. Each vinyl disc was put in each sleeve by hand.*

HOWARD DEVOTO: I think *Spiral Scratch* really turned around Buzzcocks' career. One of the reasons we did our own record was the fact we were in Manchester. There were no record companies. It wasn't like we could even find that many gigs to play. There weren't record company people coming up, the music papers weren't coming up, we had to do it ourselves. We pressed 1,000, we had no idea whether we'd even sell 1,000. We ended up selling 16,000.

The EP's running order is 'Breakdown','Times Up', 'Boredom' and 'Friends of Mine'. 'Boredom' is the standout track, with its two-note guitar solo and rumbling bass. Devoto's nasal vocal sounds like a spoof of Cockney Rebel lead singer Steve Harley.

JORDAN: Buzzcocks are still one of my favourite bands. I did a lot of gigs with them with Adam and the Ants and I thought they were great, probably the best to come out in the wake of the Pistols, and they were in a different league really. They had the same independence and the same power but they'd made something new out of it and it wasn't just a re-hash. I really didn't like the Clash very much, I think that they preached a sort of poverty-stricken, downtrodden story in their songs, nothing heroic. Just something you don't want to hear in a song, I'm afraid. I didn't like them for that. It's almost like taking being working class to its real extremes. Well the Pistols didn't need to say that, they *were* working class. If you need to state it then you've got a chip on your shoulder in some way, which is what I think separated bands like the Clash. Whereas X-Ray Spex were a great band too. They were really wonderful, I loved them and the Buzzcocks, but for a different reason. The Buzzcocks had some great lyrics and they were great guys and, do you know, I often sing their songs in the bathroom still (*laughing*).

A matter of days after Spiral Scratch hit the shops, Howard Devoto upped and left the Buzzcocks. It seemed a perverse act for a man who had achieved so much in the space of just six months. Devoto's departure from the Buzzcocks sent a genuine shock through the Manchester music scene.

There was disbelief in the music press too, but seemingly no bitterness from his bandmates. Pete Shelley, who had sung with his schoolboy band Jets of Air, took over on vocals. Four weeks later they make their live debut as the Buzzcocks – minus Howard Devoto.

PETE SHELLEY: I knew the real reason he left. He was in his final year at college and there was no future in what we were doing. It was just a bit of fun.

HOWARD DEVOTO: I felt at the time that having recorded the record, that's maybe as far as it had gone for me. I'd now seen through quite a lot of the whole process of being in a band, playing a gig and then making a record. I

Howard Devoto as lead singer of Magazine in 1977 (Photo: Granada TV)

was in the middle of my Humanities degree and, having buggered up my Psychology one and the thick end of my school career as well, I wasn't that wild to go on perpetuating my failures in the academic department. I was not fantastically taken, I suppose, with the aesthetic of it all. I wasn't that wild about the vibe and ambience of it in a way – it didn't feel exactly musically right for me at the end of January 1977. Not that I can say I was sure at that time that I'd even go on to be in another band.

But he did go on to be in another band – Magazine.

ALAN HEMPSALL (audience member): I was stood at the Elizabethan Hall, at Belle Vue (Manchester), watching Magazine's first gig. It became apparent that this man had been in a punk band but had ditched it fast. Now there was a new phase and I think that's the thing that people forget about punk. It wasn't the item in itself, it was the fact that it was a precursor to and a catalyst for what was to come. And that was the real meat and two veg. Punk had done its job, it had got rid of all the crap and the pretentiousness.

Audience member Paul Morley had, by this stage, graduated from fanzine scribbler to New Musical Express contributor, firing off despatches on the Manchester scene to London.

PAUL MORLEY: Howard Devoto seemed like an incredibly mesmeric presence. Afterwards, when he did Magazine and we wrote about him being the most important man alive, a lot of Londoners were a bit confused why we'd said this. We said it in a way, not necessarily just for the music, but because we knew that this man was responsible for bringing the Pistols up to Manchester. And that was just the beginning of everything that Manchester has since become ... even within three years it seemed important, let alone twenty-five years later.

Suddenly, across Manchester, there were places bands could play that didn't require you to be hugely famous or American. Venues like The Ranch, Pips, Rafters and the Electric Circus in Collyhurst all played their part.

PAUL MORLEY: You were going to see bands like The Fall, from Manchester, in Manchester. You were seeing Joy Division in Manchester, you were seeing Buzzcocks, you know, from Manchester, in Manchester. Suddenly you had a little scene: clearly other people that were at the two Sex Pistols concerts.

PETER HOOK: We had a meeting with Pete Shelley in a pub in Broughton (an area of Salford, Greater Manchester) to ask him how we should form a band. God, amazing! And he told us.

HOWARD DEVOTO: The Fall were pretty quick on the scene. I remember going along to the art centre and seeing them within, must have been, maybe a couple of months after that second gig.

Salford-born Mark Edward Smith formed The Fall as a bedroom band after seeing the Sex Pistols at the Lesser Free Trade Hall. Their style was a clattering marriage of psychobilly beats overlaid by Smith's often impenetrable rants. He sang of witches, bingo masters and elastic men. Baffling, yet strangely compelling.

MARK E. SMITH: We thought punk sold out very quickly and it rapidly became sped-up heavy metal bands and blokes with skinny ties. That's what got us going more. The initial promise of the Pistols wasn't really fulfilled. It went down very quickly. So we thought we'd better do something about it. The whole idea of The Fall was already being nurtured, unconsciously. It was to write intelligent lyrics to very basic music. We wanted to be a bit more esoteric. The Fall were very, very young compared to the Pistols. In a way, they became the establishment very quickly. That's what we felt at the time. When it kicked off, the thing with punk is that it was working class music. But in fact it wasn't. The Sex Pistols were on Virgin for Christ's sake – they were the enemy as far as me and my friends were concerned.

PETER HOOK: We preferred bands like The Worst; two of them, they couldn't play. One had the drum kit and one had the guitar and they just used to rant and rave. Oh, it was great. And he'd smash his kit up at the end. The second gig we did, The Worst played with us. Great days.

PAUL MORLEY: Well it happened very quickly and very naturally, there were really important bands like The Fall and the strange Warsaw/Joy Division sort of area. Even bands that seemed to sort of be crappy. There was a great band called The Worst, who were a couple of mechanics from Rochdale. They did their gigs in the same clothes they used to fix the car and the drummer had a kid's drum kit that he held together with bricks. The bass player never had his bass plugged in and, to me, they were the great lost punk group. I'd be surprised if they weren't there, at least at that second Sex Pistols show. They were fantastic and all their songs were about the police state and lasted about thirty seconds and then just disintegrated. But there were incredible bands like The Fall who happened very quickly.

ALAN HEMPSALL: I think the grimness was just something that was there in Manchester in the late Seventies. There were several ways you could deal with it and you could look at the way The Fall produced things or Joy Division, those kinds of bands. They all had a different way of portraying that. Mark E Smith and The Fall had a more tongue-in-cheek approach, more of a witty approach than Joy Division.

By the start of 1977, what began as Peter Hook and Bernard Sumner's experiment in wrecking Grandma's radiogram had developed into a band. Initially called Stiff Kittens, thanks to an idea by Buzzcocks manager Richard Boon, they settled on Warsaw, inspired by the David Bowie track 'Warsawa' on his Low *album. Ian Curtis, who had been to the second Pistols gig at the Lesser Free Trade Hall, was on vocals. Without a regular drummer, their debut was at the Electric Circus in Manchester in May of 1977, supporting the Buzzcocks and Salford 'punk poet' John Cooper Clarke. It was a measure of the scene's openness that Clarke should be 'allowed in'. He worked in the tool stores at Salford University and had long, back-combed hair. He delivery was ultra-fast and ultra-nasal. It would be hard to imagine anyone understanding a word he said outside of Manchester.*

PETER HOOK: We did a gig with the Buzzcocks at the Electric Circus and Pete Shelley said (to the audience) 'Now, stop spitting all of you please ... stop. We're not playing any more till you stop spitting.' So they all stopped. And he went, 'Right, now that's better ... one, two, three, four.' And they all spat at him! Oh God, fantastic moment in punk history. By God, it was amazing.

As 1977 turned into 1978, and with an EP called An Ideal for Living *recorded, Warsaw became Joy Division, with Steve Morris now established as permanent drummer – just as the so-called 'scene' began to separate between the punks and the post-punks.*

PAUL MORLEY: The punky, gobbie side of it was just the sort of the way it got transformed by the tabloid world, people jumping on it thinking that it was simpler and sillier than it actually was. So it kind of split very quickly into the two sides. There was that silly side that for me Slaughter and the Dogs predicted and there was the side that actually influenced all music and pop culture.

PETER HOOK: It did fragment a little bit. Tony tried his best to pull it together. God, he was the first middle class person I ever talked to, Tony Wilson. The Buzzcocks were quite middle class, so I don't think they could relate to our beer-boy attitude, when they were quite a bit art school. It was very difficult for me to sit in the same room with Howard Devoto because we absolutely had nothing in common in life apart from the fact that we were in a group. It was difficult for us as a group, because we weren't arty enough. We sort of fell out of the punk thing, it got a bit too arty, it wasn't punky enough for us.

The 'beer-boys' of Joy Division were perceived very differently by the music press. Largely through icy photographs taken of the band, they came to be seen as aloof, with a doomed grandeur. The truth couldn't be further away.

PETER HOOK: I remember the first gig we did as Joy Division, which was at Pips (former disco at Fennel Street in Manchester). That was the biggest fight I'd ever seen in my life. It was great. Every gig was just like a massive release of energy.

PAUL MORLEY: The image now tends to be the punk on King's Road with the spiky hair and the chains and the leather jackets but it was actually a really intellectual, literate movement. You think of the Buzzcocks songs that Howard Devoto wrote, they were incredibly literate. And Johnny Rotten's lyrics were incredibly literate; The Fall were incredibly literate; Joy Division, incredibly sophisticated and complex.

Other bands were appearing on the circuit too: the shouty yet disciplined Drones and Ed Banger and the Nosebleeds, who were just plain shouty.

EDDIE GARRITY: There was definitely a big change then, because we were just plodding, just doing the odd gigs up in Stalybridge and Ashton (in east Manchester) to about fifteen people. And immediately we became a punk band and had a single out, it was like four hundred people at a concert, which was like ridiculous really, 'cause no one had heard us up to that day. So being a punk band just upped the ante so much, there was so much interest in it.

After the Pistols appearance on the last episode of the series, the So It Goes *team grabbed hold of punk – and especially the new wave that was already tailing it – and bunged as many bands onto the television as possible. Out went the faffing about, in came music, music, music.*

CHRIS PYE (producer, *So It Goes*): Because we'd put the first bit of punk on television, I think there was a natural instinct that we were on a cutting edge so that we should do more of it. Punk was getting bigger.'

TONY WILSON: I waited for a year, shivering with nightmares, that someone at the BBC or elsewhere would wake up and put all these bands on. Luckily the man at the BBC thought it was all about technique, so unless you were technically proficient or American you couldn't go on the *Old Grey Whistle Test*. What a dickhead. Wonderful for us. Through the autumn and the spring of '77, we were able to put bands on at Granada: Slaughter, the Buzzcocks, the Jam and the Clash and everything. We were just very lucky that the rest of the world was dumb.

PETER WALKER: It took the development of the Sex Pistols idea and amplified it, in some cases *ad nauseum*. It became the same programme really, every week, and it was an explosion of punk which drove it. The worst highlight I remember seeing I think was Tony's idea – a thinking man's intuition about music – which Tony wanted to do and Chris wanted to do, this 'let's go down the clubs and see blokes gobbing at groups' type of programme. And of course that's what Julian Temple did, very cleverly, with the footage (from *So It Goes*). He intercut it with footage of blokes gobbing on the stage and it looked like they were performing in front of an audience. But, of course, that didn't happen, the gobbing wasn't there.

In much of the 'let's go down the clubs' footage from the second series of So It Goes, a distinctive youth can be seen clearly at the very front of the stage. Red of face – and of hair – young Mick Hucknall is unmistakable, shaking a ginger head to the likes of Siouxsie and the Banshees. By the turn of the decade he'd formed the punkish Frantic Elevators, before becoming Simply Red.

CHRIS PYE: I was a wrong generation to be sucked into it. I had a slight problem; I like harmony in music. Punk is not tremendously harmonious: there is not much three part-harmony going on. I didn't object to the violence of it or the aggression of it, I just didn't like the sound of it. I never got into it or responded to it.

Tony Wilson had, by now, started Factory Records, named after a post-punk music night at the Russell Club in Hulme. The Buzzcocks had shown with their New Hormones label that independence could be achieved. Early Factory releases came from a broad church: Durutti Column, A Certain Ratio, Joy Divison and Orchestral Manoeuvres in the Dark.

TONY WILSON: Punk created, allowed, a whole other era of music – Elvis Costello, post-punk – in which some of the high art is dropped. Joy Division, Elvis Costello or U2 doesn't happen without the flame, without the Pistols, without the explosion – without punk.

PETE SHELLEY: I think that gig (Lesser Free Trade Hall) was more or less the seed. It started a lot of things off. But of course me and Howard knew no one at all in Manchester. The only people we knew who were interested in the kind of music we were into were the Sex Pistols. I had no knowledge of the scene, if there was one. I suppose there were other people who went out but there was nothing. There was no sense of direction or purpose in it, and then suddenly there was. And it was basically 'you can do it', so everybody started doing it and surprisingly it worked out.

Other independents began to pop up, like Rabid Records, co-run by Martin Hannett, producer of Spiral Scratch. *Slaughter and the Dogs were one of their first signings and released the rockaboogie anthem 'Cranked Up Really High' as their first single. All power-chords and drawling vocals, Slaughter can still remember the day they took delivery of the first batch.*

MICK ROSSI: Just the coolest feeling in the world. I had to take it out of the sleeve, in and out about eight times, put it down, pick it up, look at it. You'd look at this piece of plastic and it would have 'Cranked Up Really High by Barrett and Rossi.' Then I'd pick up the 'Jean Jeanie' (David Bowie) … like the kid in you.

WAYNE BARRETT: For me it was like that Neil Armstrong thing, I swear to God, you know, it's a putting-a-flag-on-the-moon kind of thing.

When Joy Division's lead singer Ian Curtis committed suicide in the early hours of the 18 May 1980, the image of the band created by the press was preserved in amber for good. But it also starkly highlighted the fact that if the intensity of the music and the level of expectation was going to be this costly, then it probably wasn't worth it. Although the wave of emotion over Curtis's death made a great success of the material released afterwards, particularly the single 'Love Will Tear Us Apart', the whole scene needed to back off and re-think.

The Buzzcocks success as a pop act effectively removed them from the scene, as Pete Shelley steered them towards Top of the Pops and the charts with singles like 'What Do I Get?', 'I Don't Mind' and 'Ever Fallen in Love (With Someone You Shouldn't've)'. Their old muckers Slaughter and the Dogs had by now signed to Decca and, in a spoof of the Sex Pistols signing their contract with A&M outside Buckingham Palace, put their signatures to the deal outside Wythenshawe dole office. But away from the independent spirit of Rabid, Barrett struggled with the businesslike environment of a 'proper' record company. So he did what any Wythenshawe lad does in a tricky situation ... he did a bunk.

WAYNE BARRETT: I think it was the business side basically. For me, as an artist, I liked to dream. I like to think freely and do basically what I want. If I can't do that then it's not worth continuing. I was happy with Mike (Mick Rossi), we were the best of friends, Mr Rossi and myself. We've known each other since we were kids. Other people from the outside were coming in and destroying things. I think it became a little bit too commercial. I mean we were in it for the money as well, but we were in it for having a good time firstly. If we make money out of it then that's the reward of fame. We wanted to do just 'local famous'. When it became kind of national, people came in from the outside and started distorting it. And that's why I buggered off to France.

MICK ROSSI: At the time I was incredibly hurt. But at the same time I knew it was on the cards in a weird way, like a sixth sense type thing. Looking back on it, it's like it was a necessary evil for that to happen, because coming full circle, it's stronger and the bond is tighter than ever, which makes me happy. But at the time I was hurt.

With commitments to fulfil, Rossi found a replacement in the young man off whose head a bottle went 'ping' at the second Sex Pistols gig at the Lesser Free Trade Hall: Eddie Garrity, aka Ed Banger.

EDDIE GARRITY: I joined Slaughter in late '79 after Wayne had run off. I got a phone call and joined them within two days, because I already knew the songs from way back. Just a matter of stepping in at two days' notice and straight into the tour. We did the album and a couple of singles, but we split up again.

MICK ROSSI: It was really like, okay, who can we get? We've got to do this record, do we carry on? Yeah, I think we can carry on. What about Eddie from Ed Banger and the Nosebleeds? Eddie's a really nice man and I think it was terrific of him to step into such big shoes. It wasn't the same.

With the new Slaughter not really gelling, Rossi cast around for other collaborators. Billy Duffy, later of The

Cult, was drafted in. So was a young man who'd attended the first Free Trade Hall gig and dismissed it as 'a front parlour affair'.

MICK ROSSI: Wayne had actually gone underground, I didn't know where he was. I'd gone to another record company and started working with Billy and Billy says, 'I know this great singer called Morrisey.' So I said, okay, we'll give that a shot. So we had a few rehearsals and I felt Morrisey was incredibly talented as a lyric writer but then he was very introvert. He was this shy man, you had to prize him out of his shell, he didn't have a lot to say. Being exposed to Morrisey at his early stage, before he blossomed into what he is today, was interesting too. In a weird way it was never anything to do with Slaughter ... it was just kind of on the sideline.

Morrisey and the Dogs. Things could have been so different. Steven Patrick Morrisey – or 'the Stretford Schoolboy' as Tony Wilson still insists on calling him – would have been one of the youngest members of the audience when the Sex Pistols played in Manchester in June 1976. He went on to front The Smiths, probably the most important group of the 1980s. He had already been a temporary member of an Ed Banger-less Nosebleeds before his link up with Slaughter. It seems mighty strange now to think that the fey wordsmith who would invite you to 'pin and mount me like a butterfly' in The Smith's song 'Reel Around the Fountain' once held his own with south Manchester toughs like Slaughter and the Nosebleeds. It's an indication, if nothing else, of his willingness to succeed at all costs.

With guitarist and co-writer Johnny Marr (yet another

Wythenshawe boy), Morrisey's swooning, literate tales of graveyard walks, back alley fumblings and hopeless infatuation made a generation reach for the smelling salts. Piled high with expectation and weighed down by internal dissatisfaction, drugs and money wrangles, The Smiths collapsed in 1987, much to the indignation of their followers. Their albums stand the test of time better than any artists of the period and their influence can be traced to today via bands like The Sundays, Gene, Marion and Coldplay. Johhny Marr, who copped for the blame at the time of the split, became a guitar for hire and went on to work with Bernard Sumner in Electronic. Morrisey's fitful solo career has always suffered from comparison with the band's work. He now lives in America, wary of speaking to journalists to the point of reclusiveness. When his representatives in the States were contacted to seek his involvement in I Swear I Was There, they didn't actually know where he was. He'd 'taken off somewhere'.

Joy Division's answer for the need to be relieved of the weighty expectation that surrounded them was to become New Order ... and to dance. After initially testing the water as a three-piece, drummer Stephen Morris's girlfriend Gillian Gilbert was recruited and they had their first hit with 'Ceremony' in 1981.

The following year saw an inspirational visit to New York, with the idea to bring an NYC disco to the grey streets of Manchester. Inspired by clubs like the Danceteria, The Funhouse and The Paradise Garage, New Order and Factory Records found an ex-boat showroom on Whitworth Street West and turned it into The Hacienda. Its grey and yellow interior was designed by Ben Kelly, who also helped create interiors at a shop at 430 King's Road in London, former business address of one Malcolm McLaren. Using the subtitle of 'FAC 51', as it was the fifty-first thing produced by Factory, it opened on 21 May 1982. Stars of the day like Martin Fry of ABC and Ian McCulloch of Echo and the Bunnyman were there on that fateful evening. Sadly, it was crap.

Nobody used to go to the Hacienda in its early, pre-dance phase. The sound was awful, the silvery-paint came off on your clothes and you could only get in with a credit-card style membership thing, which all the wreckheads promptly lost immediately after being issued them. My friends and I used to go to the Hacienda some Saturday nights if we were tired and wanted somewhere to have a sit down. As a gig venue, it just about got away with it, with some key performances by The Smiths and New Order. The rest of the time it was the likes of proto-Goths Bauhaus, The Birthday Party and McLaren protégés Bow Wow Wow that filled the ticket. I know. I paid for them.

But the Hacienda was saved thanks to the other thing that New Order brought back from New York along with the idea of a big, flouncey discotheque in the middle of Manchester. Electro beats. Big shiny ones that you could see your face in ... and dance your arse off to. New Order jettisoned everything bar Peter Hook's low-slung bass lines in favour of sequencers, drum machines and spidery, one-finger synthesiser melodies. Using Kraftwerk via Africa Bambaataa, they made it okay for white boys to dance. A vital leap.

With the release of the album Power, Corruption and Lies, and of the 12-inch electro work-out 'Blue Monday' in 1983, New Order also helped keep the doors of the ailing Hacienda open. 'Blue Monday' spent over thirty weeks in the charts, became the best-selling 12-inch single of all time and provided a financial prop to the club that bridged the lean years before acid house and rave culture made The Hacienda and Madchester the place to be. It also proved that the hitherto sexually and culturally incompatible bedfellows of rock and dance could do it together.

Dance nights at The Hacienda took over as the most popular events, pushing the rock boys elsewhere. A barely-used counselling drug, 3,4-methylenedioxymethamphetamine, or MDMA, became the stimulant of choice. The baby-acid drug known as ecstasy made everything sound great and everyone seem REALLY great. The Happy Mondays, essentially Slaughter and the Dogs on ecstasy, came up with the album Bummed, *produced by Martin Hannett. Stone Roses cleverly swerved their gothic past with the help of a 'Funky Drummer' beat. And former Factory signing James got everyone to Sit Down ... but only after you've bought their tee-shirts. Oh – and the Inspiral Carpets were keen for you to buy theirs too.*

Rock and dance had come together and formed a coalition. Without that truce, the connection to the Lesser Free Trade Hall would have been severed and the seeds sown by the Pistols would have died with the closure of The Hacienda prior to the dance boom. The appropriation of shiny beats by two lads who started out on Grandma's stereo after seeing the Sex Pistols in 1976 had saved the day. Manchester's stranglehold on popular music and its attached culture was able to continue in the 1990s. When, ironically, the beats were replaced by the dull thud of distorted guitars.

TONY WILSON: Youth cultural revolutions – for me, they're the greatest things. There was an old sound guy at Granada in Manchester, who was a lovely old geezer, he once said to me, 'I went to record the Beatles at the Cavern, in late '62. I've got the tape of it.' He brought the tape in of the Beatles in the Cavern, in '62. And you know what it sounded just like? The Pistols at the Free Trade Hall in '76. It's got that energy and reality. Whenever there's a youth revolution, the people in charge of the media have grown up in the last one: 'This is quite interesting, but not as good as the last one.' That's bollocks, they're all equally valuable. Acid house was as good as punk and punk was as good as Merseybeat. They're all fantastic moments of renewal.

7: A Girl of About 18, Wearing Glasses

IN WHICH THE PLAYERS DISCUSS HOW THE SEX PISTOLS
CHANGED THE SHAPE OF ROCK AND THE AUTHOR FEELS
THE NEED TO CONFESS.

WHEN OASIS experienced their first rush of success, one wag coined a nickname for the inexplicably popular band from Burnage. The Sex Beatles. And that just about sums up the way events of 1976 in Manchester changed the shape of rock. Noel and Liam Gallagher would have been aged nine and four at the time, but even after the fact, they got it. And thus became part of it. Never Mind the Bollocks – Here's the Sex Pistols *is Noel Gallagher's joint-favourite album of all time, along with the 'Blue' and 'Red' Beatles best-of compilations. It's a system of connections that works in a similar way to the movie brainteaser 'Six Degrees of Kevin Bacon', whereby you have to make a link between any given film and the carrot-topped* Footloose *fellow in less than half a dozen moves. The chain of events started on June 4, 1976, was to shape Manchester music. The city has always been the nation's tastemaker in terms of popular culture. For 'Manchester music' you can take it as read, in fact, that we are talking about 'British music'. In 1986, a music festival was held in Manchester marking a decade of influence following the Sex Pistols performance at the Lesser Free Trade Hall. The climax of the 'Festival of the Tenth Summer' was a gig by The Fall, New Order and The Smiths, bands who were all links in the chain that drags us back to that auditorium on Peter Street in Manchester.*

PAUL MORLEY: Funnily enough, I've often done it for practice: join the line from the Sex Pistols all the way up to Mr Scruff and Badly Drawn Boy. Everything that happens in Manchester is still a fall-out of the Sex Pistols coming to the Lesser Free Trade Hall. There's no doubt about it – all the way through Joy Division to the Stone Roses, from The Fall to Happy Mondays, all the way through to the dance stuff, anything mad that happened at the Hacienda, you can all draw it back to that little explosion at the Lesser Free Trade Hall. It's not hard at all.

TONY WILSON: The success of Manchester is in not being the typical city like Bristol, which has a good three years, or Seattle, which has a good three years, or Liverpool, which has a good three years. Manchester having a good twenty years begins that night on June the fourth and it's as if you can use the phrase 'being set into motion'. The spin that was created that night lasted until probably Oasis. It went for a long time. Something about the energy imparted that night set up a train of events which takes us through to today. Factory Records would not have existed and my life would not have been what it was without Joy Division. And Joy Division got up on stage because they saw these buggers (Sex Pistols) on stage. Well if they can do it, we can do it. That was the message.

WAYNE BARRETT: I like Oasis. I'm sure they have the same kind of record collection as ours, apart from them

Joy Division making a rare television appearance (Photo: Granada TV)

having a lot more Beatles than we did. But I like the character, I do like the character of the two brothers. They show the talent, the aggresivity of the Mancunian person. No Londoner or no Scotsman or Irishman or whatever could take that away from the Mancunian. That's his sincerity. It might come out in a strange way but what he says is what he believes in.

MICK ROSSI: There's certain breeding you get being in Manchester. It's kind of in your blood, especially if you're into music. It just kind of crawls in, I think, naturally. I would agree, I think Noel Gallagher is a genius – absolutely fantastic. I love Oasis.

IAN MOSS: Much as I loved David Bowie and Roxy Music and Iggy Pop and Lou Reed, there was no way that I could have envisaged meeting those people or having anything to say to those people. With the Sex Pistols, all those barriers were down. Everybody was the same, you were as important as the band, right from the start it was obvious that the rock star facade didn't exist. That was radical. Even the tinniest most pathetic bands, the first thing they did probably before they learned to play was preen in a mirror and play at being a rock star. That was probably the most radical thing, to do away with that star system and all that nonsense, that we are better than the audience.

If you have bought this book, I think we can take it as read that you are pretty serious about rock music. That is something that is sneered at in some quarters. It's Only Rock and Roll, *after all. Jesus, I hate that expression. Because, as the Sex Pistols' appearances at the Lesser Free Trade Hall show, rock music can actually change things. Granted, it tends to change items and areas of popular culture that have a link with it, but it changes things nonetheless. Most importantly, it changes* people. *It can turn an accountant into an artist, a council worker into a rock star or TV presenter into a record mogul.*

And the people who were there, at the Lesser Free Trade Hall, definitely experienced a change.

PAUL MORLEY: The great thing about the Sex Pistols show was, physically and mentally, they were like us and they were doing something themselves. You thought, it can be done, you don't have to learn an instrument in that conventional way, you don't have to write in that conventional way. They liberated you to be able to do it in a way that for Britain and for me was absolutely brand new. I always think of the great punk spirit being more like surrealism or Dadaism. There's a tendency for people to look back on it and think of the gobbing and the safety pins. It was much more of an artistic kind of release and it was a continuation of surrealism, rather than it just gave you a chance to stick a safety pin through your cheek and gob on people.

PETE SHELLEY: I don't think it's just by chance that all these unknown people have gone to a gig and then suddenly all these people were all celebrated in one way or another. The chances of that happening, you know, choosing a random room . . . People must have felt, I can do that.

IAN MOSS: Everything in Manchester that had any cultural significance, to this day, you can trace in some way back to the Sex Pistols playing at the Lesser Free Trade Hall. There would have been no Joy Division without the Sex Pistols. There would have been no Factory Records, therefore no Hacienda. In Manchester's cultural heritage over the last twenty-five years, that was the start of it. That made people go out and do things and believe that they could go out and do things and create things.

ALAN HEMPSALL: When I saw the Pistols, it took me a year until I joined a band. I wanted to be in a band but didn't have the discipline to learn an instrument. Be a singer – that would be easier. I met up with these people and, unfortunately, none of them had seen the Pistols. They were very much 'old school' with the long hair and the 'let's have guitar solos'. I got fired after three months because I couldn't actually sing. So I decided if I formed my own band, I couldn't get fired.

TONY WILSON: Whenever you see a band and you've got that look in the seventeen-year-old's eyes, that they're not

Tony Wilson today: 'The spin that was created that night lasted
until probably Oasis' (Photo: Ian Cartwright)

on that stage because they want to be pop stars, they want
to make music ... They're on stage because they have no
fucking choice, which is what all great bands look like, be
that the Pistols or Joy Division.

*We may have left it a little late into the proceedings for
this, but I'm afraid I wasn't there. I was a few years too
young. But I've always been fascinated by the idea of being
in places at a time when, in years ahead, people would
actually be interested to hear your recollections; that your
very presence becomes part of the narrative. My friend
Peter Oldham, who took the photographs used in this book
is, I suspect, slightly baffled by the way I've held a torch for
this for so long. It's because it matters ... It matters that the
date on the ticket was wrong, that the Buzzcocks were*

replaced by Howard's mate Geoff's progressive rock band, that Shelley and Devoto nearly got a good hiding to keep them off the bill at the second gig and it matters that we now know who Gentlemen are.

The problem is, I don't know why it matters. It just does, okay?

To those who understand this, detail and facts count for a great deal. Who, what, when, where, why are paramount. If I am ever asked the 'what was the first gig you ever went to?' question, the reply I give is always delivered quick as a shot, without hesitation, no problemo: XTC – Manchester Polytechnic All Saints' Building, 1978. And every time it happens, I inwardly release a little guilt hormone into myself. Not enough to double myself up, just a twinge. Because, in my heart of hearts, I actually know it was 1979. Very early 1979 mind you. Don't get me wrong. It's just that 1978 sounds so much better.

I believe that this is a fairly common problem.

I suppose it's because 1978 is a step closer to 1977. Which is a step closer still to 1976. Or 1076, if your to believe the hand-printed lettering on the ticket of that first Pistols gig at the Lesser Free Trade Hall.

In 1979, I had just turned my hair bleach blond. On the night of my first gig I had PVC trousers on as I waited outside the Polytechnic to see XTC. I stood on my tiptoes inside my zip-up boots to make myself taller and thus improve my chances of getting in ... because it was an over-18's only venue and I was only 14.

After I did get in, I only have three memories of the entire event. I can remember that the wall behind the stage had a mural of Dennis the Menace and Gnasher on it. I can remember that at one stage a skinhead pushed lead singer Andy Partridge away from the microphone and took over vocal duties himself. And I can remember that a girl of about 18, wearing glasses, allowed me to hold her jumper-

covered breasts from behind during the encores. Oh yes ... and I remember being sick the whole of the following day because of the amount of alcohol I had consumed. About three and a half pints. Despite this, to this day I genuinely believe that beer tastes best drunk from a plastic pint pot. The kind they serve at gigs.

Not a ground-breaking event, you might say. They're unlikely to make a documentary or publish a book about that, you might add. I hear what you're saying. But still, not bad for a 14-year-old from Altrincham at his first ever gig. What can I say – you know, that's what '78 was like. Sorry. 1979.

The reason I bring it up is because the other thing that has always fascinated me is people's recollections of events that would lead anyone to say I Swear I Was There.

TONY WILSON: If you talk to Mark E Smith, talk to Hooky (Peter Hook) or Barney (Bernard Sumner), or any of them, it was all like, Oh my God, the Pistols were fantastic because (a) it was fantastic, and (b) they just got on stage. So the idea that you needed to be special or you needed to have £5,000 worth of synthesisers and be Rick Wakeman or need a music degree – all that bollocks – was just removed, got rid of.

The stories surrounding the three events described here – the first and second gigs at the Lesser Free Trade Hall and the Pistols performance on So It Goes – are touched upon in every book about the Sex Pistols and British punk rock ever written. Yet at every turn of research, a new lead appears, a new connection, a new contradiction. The same stories are trotted out, but rarely is anyone who was actually there actually asked what actually happened. When you do ask, it becomes like the fable of the blind men feeling an elephant ... each coming up with a totally different impression from their contact with a slightly different part of the animal. And how do you actually remember stuff, with accuracy, a quarter of a century on from those non-sighted pachyderm fumblings?

We'll never know. And although some of the testimony in the book may be unintentionally misleading, or may suffer from my 1978 XTC syndrome, it has been fun editing it. And it's great that Howard Devoto can't resist a dig at Slaughter and the Dogs in the foreword – even after all this time.

Can it be overstated how important the Lesser Free Trade Hall is to Manchester music? At the time of writing, Manchester's listings magazine City Life *is planning a 'Festival of the 25th Summer' to mark the quarter of a century that has elapsed since the Pistols played a bunch of cover versions and a smattering of their own songs in a little theatre above the hall named after a political movement. It will be made up of interconnected events: gigs, films exhibitions and what Howard Devoto might call 'existential happenings'. If people are going to that amount of trouble, it must have been important.*

PETER HOOK: The thing that shapes Manchester music – is Manchester. Manchester did it themselves – and to my mind, we actually did it better. Manchester is a fantastic musical place and sometimes, when I look back at how many bands have come out of Manchester and how important they are, it's just unbelievable.

TONY WILSON: When Manchester celebrated the dawn of the millennium, after the fanfare at midnight, the first minute of 2000, what song did they play? In the main arena, to the 10,000 people dancing up and down, they played 'Hey Jude'. In Manchester. Doesn't mean you've got to be stupid, right? The Beatles from Liverpool, the Rolling Stones from London. Doesn't matter where it comes from. Doesn't matter that the Pistols were London, that's not important. We played our part – they played their part. It's a wonderful, wonderful world.

The one question that was put to every interviewee was: are we over-exaggerating this in terms of importance? Was this really as important as it's made out to be, or are we just shitting this up into something it isn't? Interestingly, one of the few dissenting voices was former Sex Pistol Glen Matlock. And we know he was definitely there.

GLEN MATLOCK: What, the good old days, and all that? Well, a bit of that ... But I think there was a sea change. But I don't think that, because we did what we did then, that was the cause of it. I think people were looking for stuff.

Which, put another way, is it's not so much that the Pistols were so fantastic, it is that the alternatives available at the time were so deeply unfantastic. And that made the band seem impossibly attractive, glamorous even.

I do believe that people like the idea of the Sex Pistols considerably more than they do the reality. I know of few people who get home and slap on their copy of Never Mind the Bollocks. *More likely, the attraction lies in the fact that the name Sex Pistols still carries a shudder-value with it, even after all this time. Yet the source of their notoriety – wearing unusual clothes and swearing on the television – is mild compared to the 'antics' of bands of today like Slipknot and Cradle of Filth. Yet these are seen as panto acts, a bit of fun. In 1976/77, the Pistols seemed like a genuine threat to society merely because everything else was so unthreatening. And it was a great story.*

But let's put it into perspective. It was four lads playing pretty good rock and roll.

Which is all that Slaughter and the Dogs were trying to do. Slaughter have taken a lot of stick over the years, mainly because of the 'glam' thing. Yes, it's true – both Wayne Barrett and Mick Rossi were wearing what can only be described as 'blouses' for the second gig. And yes, their bass player had hair that stretched down to the bottom of his rib cage. But that makes them no different to a hundred other bands who headed for the barbers in the wake of punk rock. If anything, they were earlier than most.

MICK ROSSI: The aim after the Free Trade Hall thing was for us to try and hit London. We had a few false starts but we finally got there. We started to realise what was going on.

WAYNE BARRETT: When we went down to London, that's when we did tidy up our look. No more ironing, no more satin, things like that. The brown thing I was wearing at the Free Trade Hall, I think it was my mum who made that.

How punk rock is that? But punk is an easy word to throw around. It's sticks to a lot of cultural flypaper, most of the time inappropriately. But it's down to the beholder: the kid in Baltimore with an Offspring CD in the back of his baggy shorts knows exactly what it means. So does the forty-something Stiff Little Fingers fan in Anytown, UK. To cover that amount of ground, punk must have made an awful lot of connections to many, many people. All we need is a reason. Plus, of course, a dissenting voice.

HOWARD DEVOTO: I think, as it transpired, that the immediacy of being in a punk group – the whole thing of, well we can hardly play, but here we are on stage and we're writing this song as we're playing it, and it's going to be over in thirty seconds – that was kind of setting yourself off against the kinds of things you'd be seeing in pubs. Which would either be earnest folk rock stuff or prog rock stuff, where people were trying to be flash and heavy with as much heavy equipment as they could manage. Punk did try and take over all aspects of music – where you played, how your records looked, the whole thing of suddenly everybody had to have a picture disc, the way people looked, the way they related to the music business, the kind of music they played. One attempted to try and change everything. That isn't to say that some people didn't kind of still come up through pub rock. I mean, punk became a very wide church with all kinds of rabble.

TONY WILSON: There is a bit of cultural theory from my dear guitarist, Vinnie Reilly (Durutti Column – he was also briefly in Ed Banger and the Nosebleeds) to explain punk and the development of the Pistols. Punk not only changed culture, it actually radicalised music in terms of melody, chords and modality. We hippie kids from the Sixties and early Seventies, we learn the guitar and you learn chords that play the one, four, five, tonal development which is what Twentieth Century western music is based around. You learn C ... F ... G7. If you couldn't play guitar at all you'd just play an F chord, an F shape. Suddenly if you can't play at all, and you're doing this bar chord, you go up and down. You watch any punk band. So suddenly melody was freed from the constraints of the previous twenty years, that is why it freed melody and allowed new melodic things to happen and why it sounded so fresh. That's not me, that's Vinnie my guitarist telling me that.

JORDAN: I think the most important part of it is, it empowered the youth of that time to do their own thing. It sounds kind of corny to say 'to rebel against their parents'. They felt a camaraderie, if you like. People were drawn together in big gangs, but not necessarily aggressive gangs. The press wanted to make out that it was much like the mods and rockers. They tried to incite violence between, say, the skinheads and punks, because they didn't want it all to be peaceful and happy. The youth were empowered to be their own man or woman – and that's another thing as well, the sexes weren't quite so separated during that time. You wouldn't see girls going to clubs dressing up just to please men. They dressed up to please themselves and in a way it was a sort of sexual revolution because nobody was playing games with anybody. You dressed up to look great whether you were a man or a woman and there was no role-playing.

WILL BIRCH (Author: *No Sleep Till Canvey Island – The Great Pub Rock Revolution*): I don't think the Sex Pistols were musically of any interest at all. I think the lyrics were tremendous and I think Johnny Rotten's vocal style was great – hugely entertaining. I think the whole Sex Pistols image and the way they launched themselves in London was so outrageous, was fantastic. But as far as the music was concerned – I don't want to come across as a muso, because I hope I'm not a muso – but their actual backing was really bog standard. There was nothing new about it at all. But I think they were about the only one of those punk rock groups of the early half dozen or so big names that did that kind of 'pushing against the beat' thing that the Stones or the Faces would do. That was tremendously old-fashioned. They did that and they got away with it. The Clash would never do that, or the Buzzcocks or The Ramones.

The achievements of the Buzzcocks are extraordinary, not only in their organisation of both gigs – although Malcolm McLaren clearly took over the second time, otherwise they wouldn't have walked off with only £10 – but in their production of Spiral Scratch, *the first independent record produced by a 'punk' band. To hear Pete Shelley speak about these events, he could almost be a addressing a motivational business seminar, albeit in a very soft voice.*

PETE SHELLEY: It seemed an impossible dream. We didn't realise it was as simple as just doing it. And when you did it, people thought, Oh, they're doing it ... so lots of people realised they could do it. People were saying, 'I'm a writer.' Instead of people saying, 'No you're not,' they believed them and let them get on with writing.

The story of the Pistols first appearance on television – on So It Goes – *shows how a triumph can get snatched from the jaws of chaos. It's remarkable that Glen Matlock was not even aware that there were other bands on the programme. Having said that, they were ensconced in a dressing room arguing about Jordan's armband. The following series of* So It Goes *changed out of all recogni-*

tion from the pseudo-comedy show that the Pistols found themselves on. It provided not only a record of bands like The Clash, Penetration and Siouxsie and the Banshees but laid the foundations for a music television format that would be picked up by the likes of The Tube.

For the purposes of this book, I took Glen Matlock into the studio where he made his first television appearance in 1976. ' Yeah,' he said.' I remember this. There was seats over there ... ' He then recalled calling Tony Wilson a cunt.

GLEN MATLOCK: To me, music is communicating with people. Music is picking up a guitar and playing in front of somebody and getting some feedback straight away. I'm not a Luddite. I've got a computer system at home and all that, I can do all that. It's what you choose to do with it that is another matter, but it's so laborious and it's so slow. It's a joke. With a guitar you go 'de de ... ' Something's happening straight away, it's more immediate. That's why I like it. If you don't relate to people, it's just wanking.

For the majority of Britain, the 1960's didn't actually start until 1971: the hair, the paisley, the clothes, let alone the faintest whiff of free sex or non-prescription drugs. By the same token, the Sex Pistols had gone by the time most people tagged onto what was happening. And they'd become a panto by then anyway, falling in under the weight of the idea that Sid Vicious was in any way capable of being the figurehead of the band.

So, the events in Manchester in the summer of 1976 were a lot of things. Inspiring – obviously. Iconic – definitely. Clouded by mists and mirrors as to what the truth about them really was – totally.

As Pete Shelley says: 'There's a lot of unanswered ques-

tions about those gigs – might have been something in the beer, I don't know.'

PETE SHELLEY: It certainly grabbed people's attention. And they think, oh yeah, it doesn't have to be the way that stops me doing things, it can be the way in which it enables me to do things. Just depends whether the glass is half empty or half full, or if there's time to go out and buy a bottle.

HOWARD DEVOTO: I know that it changed my life beyond a whole roomful of shadows of doubt – forever.

The main thing – and the reason that it's really important – is that it's a strange tale, the kind that leads to an inevitable myth. Two young guys see an article, travel to London, organise a gig and that gig changes the shape of their lives and the shape rock. Then lots of people say, I Swear I Was There.

It's important because, if nothing else, it's a great story.

8: One-Seventeenth of it is Punk Rock

IN WHICH WE INQUIRE AS TO THE WHEREABOUTS
OF OUR CAST OF PLAYERS.

MUCH HAS happened to the cast of players in the twenty-five years since the Sex Pistols took to the stage of the Lesser Free Trade Hall in Manchester and changed the shape of rock. The Pistols themselves split after their show at the Winterland Ballroom in San Francisco in January 1978, at the end of a seven-date tour of entirely inappropriate cities and venues in the American South. Glen Matlock 'left' the group with a mighty £3,000, to be replaced by Sid Vicious. Who died. Shortly after Nancy died. Eighteen years after the Winterland split, the original Pistols reformed to play gigs in Europe, America, Australia, New Zealand, Japan and South America.

Glen Matlock formed Rich Kids in 1977 with Steve New and Rusty Egan. Midge Ure joined shortly afterwards and they spent five weeks in the charts the following year with their eponymous power-pop anthem 'Rich Kids'. They made one album, Ghosts of Princes in Towers *and managed the difficult, three-way trick of being in at the start of New*

Glen Matlock now tours with his band The Philistines: 'Songwriting is a craft you learn and hone as you get older.' (Photo: Rachel Joseph)

Wave, prefiguring much of the mist-shrouded imagery of the New Romantics ... and not being very successful.

GLEN MATLOCK: It's the way of the rock business. At the time, I think they (Rich Kids) paved the way for lots of other bands – the Skids, people like the Eurythmics. Even those girls who ended up in (singing) 'Don't You Want Me Baby' (Human League), they were down the front of our gigs. The rock business is never a big sea change, there's always a little bit of this and a little bit of that. It kind of teeters forward from one thing to the next.

He's since worked with the likes of Jackie Leven, former lead singer with Scottish New Wave/folk nutcases Doll by Doll and toured with his band The Philistines. They released an album called Open Mind *in 2000, which got healthy reviews.*

GLEN MATLOCK: Is that surprising? People think that you do something and then you just totally forget how to do anything associated with it. But songwriting is a craft and you learn and hone as you get a bit older. I try and keep my ear to the ground and finger on the pulse of what's going on. Whether you choose to do that or not – follow the trend – I personally choose not to. Other people do that. I think I'm as contemporary as the next bloke but it's just people's perceptions. People actually like what I'm doing. I've written some good songs in the past and I will continue to write songs, so you shouldn't be so surprised.

Today, Matlock cuts a trim, geezer-ish figure whose gor-blimey voice and tendency to wear daytime shades distract from him being an ordinary bloke who's lived through extraordinary times. This is the man who read in print that Pistols guitarist Steve Jones once wanked into a stick of French bread, then offered it to him to eat – but still agreed to tour with him on the reunion tour. He has put up with a great deal of abuse from the other Pistols, especially John Lydon (Rotten). Today, Rotten lives in America, has an internet radio show and refuses to talk about the 1970s and punk rock.

Matlock was the youngest Pistol, but only by a matter of months. Today, he looks years younger than the others. A female colleague who sat in during our talk described him as 'the only actually sexy Pistol'. Glen is currently playing with Dead Men Walking, a project which also features Pete Wylie (The Mighty Wah!), Mike Peters (The Alarm) and Kirk Brandon (Theatre of Hate).

GLEN MATLOCK: What do you do, crawl under a stone, just 'cos it suits everybody else? Fuck that. I've come to the conclusion that you can't please everybody, so you might as well please yourself. I keep writing all the time anyway and I've got sackfuls and sackfuls of songs. I mean, some of them are cobblers but some of them are good. So there's no point in them being in a cassette in your bottom drawer. I heard that Ronnie Spector was looking for some material and sat down, wrote a song with this friend of mine, a girl called Patti Palladin, who used to work with Johnny Thunders, sent her a song and she's doing it.

Howard Devoto now lives in East London and works as a photo archive director. With his close-cropped hair and heavy black spectacles, he looks a little like New Wave singer Joe Jackson and ex-footballer Nobby Stiles – only with a degree in Humanities. Far from his enigmatic image, he is keen and able to talk about events of 1976 and beyond. The band he formed when he left the Buzzcocks, Magazine, were probably the purest statement of the New Wave. They took the edge but left behind the posturing. They kept the distorted guitars but overlaid them with clean keyboard lines. They prefigured both the cold detachment of the New Romantics and the psychedelic swirl of the Liverpool groups that would dominate the early 1980s: Echo and the Bunnymen and The Teardrop Explodes. The group also acted as an extraordinary Job Centre for other bands to poach personnel from and created even more complex connections to the Sex Pistols and that night of June 4 at the Lesser Free Trade Hall. Magazine guitarist John McGeogh went on to join Siouxsie and the Banshees. Sid Vicious was an early member of the Banshees. Vicious of course replaced Glen Matlock in the Pistols in February 1977. McGeogh later joined Public Image Limited with Johnny Rotten/Lydon. Magazine bass player Barry Adamson and keyboardist Dave Formula joined Steve Strange's Visage project, which also included Midge Ure – who'd previously been in Rich Kids with Glen Matlock. Incestuous times. Now, twenty-five years on, things have come full circle for Howard Devoto.

HOWARD DEVOTO: In some kind of curious turn of events, Pete Shelley and myself have found ourselves working together again. There's computers – you don't sit around with a guitar anymore in your front room. You still sit around in your front room, but it's with a computer more than a guitar. It's actually fantastic to work with him again. He and I have not really worked together since 1977, some time after *Spiral Scratch* and I'd left the band. We hadn't even particularly seen that much of each other, maybe once every two or three years. Suddenly, we're seeing each other every week. It's great to be getting to know him again, but more than that, I really do like the music we're doing. I'm just beginning to see the real shape. It doesn't sound to me like what either of us have done quite before. There again, I don't think it'll be a huge surprise. That there's a kind of aggression to it, is still important to me. Do people understand that word 'edge' any more? I don't, awful word ... let's talk about resonance. No, definitely won't talk about resonance. Hell, I don't know, I mean it ain't punk rock, I'll tell you that. Well apart from a little bit. A little bit of it's punk rock – about one-seventeenth of it is punk rock.

Howard Devoto today: 'enigmatic but mad as a brush'.
(Photo: Granada TV)

When Pete Shelley continued with Buzzcocks after Devoto's departure, he created a body of albums – and particularly singles – that generated hits and affection in equal measure. But by 1981 the band had split, only to reform by the end of the decade, with a full-on comeback in 1993 with the album Trade Test Transmissions. *In between he worked with the Invisible Girls and released material under the heading of the Tiller Girls. As a solo artist, his 1982 album* Homosapien *was a well-received slice of electro-pop that was completely of its time. Today, softly spoken, smiling gently and blonder than Jordan was a quarter of a century ago, Pete is still playing music.*

PETE SHELLEY: I'm working with Howard Devoto – under the working title 'Buzzkunst'. Even though I was twenty-one when it all happened (punk rock) it seems a long time ago, but strangely quite recent. I always thought that twenty-five years is a very, very long time. We did a show at the ICA recently, we did four songs. We've now got about a dozen, so we're putting them together, hopefully to be released in the New Year. It's been really good working with Howard because, in some ways, I'd forgotten about how mad he was in the first place. At the start of Buzzcocks, you always think of Howard as being very enigmatic. But really, he's as mad as a brush.

For Tony Wilson, Factory Records and the Hacienda are no more. He now runs the Red Cellars record label and an internet music site. He still presents programmes for Granada Television, including Soccer Brain *and* The Sport Exchange. *In January 2001, work started on a feature film chronicling Wilson's life and times called* 24 Hour Party People. *Wilson is played by comedian Steve Coogan. One of the key early scenes of the film is Wilson at the Lesser Free Trade Hall in 1976, watching the Sex Pistols.*

TONY WILSON: That's quite an important moment in the movie and I hope they get it right. In the original screenplay it was like everyone pogoing and jumping up and down and it was a riot. And you go, well actually you can do that because a lot of the movie's not real, you can be unreal. But the reality is, there was no pogoing. Pogo really hadn't been invented at that point. The people who were there were just sitting, in these chairs just ... gobsmacked.

I became involved – and thought it was a good idea – about three years ago. It's like a *Boogie Nights* concept. The dawn of punk to the death of acid, taking you through two revolutions on their up and down cycles. That's really interesting and hopefully the movie will get over the feel of these moments, although the film has resolved itself into being not really about the music. It's more a comedy about a bunch of idiots, which is me and my mates. A black comedy, because quite a few people die in it.

One of the characters in the 24 Hour Party People *film is Hooky – Peter Hook. He is played in the film by actor Ralf Little, Anthony in the BBC's* The Royle Family. *After recording one album under the name* Revenge, *Hook formed Monaco with tape operator David Potts.*

PETER HOOK: I'm working with Monaco, we're doing very well, really enjoying it, really good. New Order are at it again, we're halfway through an LP, which is going to be finished for 2001.

Pete Shelley, back working with Howard Devoto after more
than 20 years (Photo: Granada TV)

*Hook now shares a record label with a rock legend who
goes back much further than a mere twenty-five years – Sir
Cliff Richard. Sir Cliff has one thing in common with the Sex
Pistols. They were both 'let go' by the same record
company, EMI. Peter is full of support for the Peter Pan of
Pop. Perhaps because, like Johnny Rotten, Cliff means it ...
man.*

PETER HOOK: Cliff got dropped from EMI, which is a
very sad comment on the way the world goes. He'd been with
EMI for years, must have made them millions and millions
of pounds. He came up with the idea of doing 'The Lord's

175

Prayer', which is quite a punky idea. It's only like Crass (anar-cho-punk band) when they did the same thing. They wouldn't release it so he turned to these two guys at Papillon Records. They couldn't believe EMI could ditch an established artist who had made music for so long. Whether you like it or not is not the point, there's supposed to be some loyalty in the world. They (Papillon) put it out and with the success they had off Cliff Richard, they've gone round sorting out the bands that have been dropped by major record companies to make way for all these boy bands. They've signed the Human League – very early punk band – Terrorvision, World Party and Monaco. It's really nice to be with a label, after twenty-five years, where the guys love music and aren't being greedy. That to me is what punk's all about. So I'm happy to be back full circle on an independent label.

Mark E. Smith, the young man who worked for the docks, formed The Fall a year after seeing the Sex Pistols. The job he created for himself in 1977 is the job he holds today – lead singer of The Fall. It's possible that anyone who owns a musical instrument and lives in the Greater Manchester area has, at some point, been in The Fall. He's produced so many albums that compilers balk at the task of annotating them. His acerbic reputation travels so far ahead of him, it arrives the day before your meeting is due to take place. And demands a drink. When he was interviewed for this book he drank many Budweisers, but could not be more charming. He is a nice, somewhat frail man, who holds a unique place in British rock: that of a vague conscience.

MARK E. SMITH: We still feel very much outside the music business. The group's a lot younger than me now, which is a big improvement ... lot more spunk, you know?

I'm trying to get more into that 'spoken word' thing. It's looking better than it has for a good five years now. Every time I leave a record company, they bring a bloody compilation out, you just get all these 'retros'. Which is why I'm a bit down on this kind of thing. I don't look very far ahead, that's my problem. I don't look more than six months ahead. I would have a marvellous job in shipping if it weren't for the Sex Pistols. I'd probably have my own shipping company, worldwide! Many times I've cursed the Sex Pistols!

Audience member Alan Hempsall went on to form his own band in 1978, called Crispy Ambulance. After releasing a single on their own Aural Assault label, they signed to Tony Wilson's Factory Records. And to add to the increasingly convoluted connections to the Lesser Free Trade Hall, he once stood in for Joy Division frontman Ian Curtis after the epileptic singer suffered a particularly violent seizure.

ALAN HEMPSALL: About a month before he died he was a bit off colour for a performance, so I got the call and stood in for him at this at this particular gig at Bury Town Hall. And a very eventful evening it was too. It had sold out fairly quickly, the momentum of Joy Division had well and truly built up, 'Love will Tear Us Apart' was in the can and was about two months away from being released. I knew the stuff and they just said, 'Well, pick whatever you know the words to.' So it was great, just pick your favourite Joy Division songs and away we go. We then play 'Love Will Tear Us Apart' and 'Digital'. I then go off the stage, Ian Curtis then comes on and he felt well enough to do two very slow numbers. Then we all leave and we leave a very confused audience. There was this loud crash and as we'd walked off some wag had just picked up an empty bottle and lobbed it at this enormous glass chandelier suspended over the stage, sending shards of glass showering as we were walking off. Tony Wilson was by the door, and I can just hear all these bottles breaking against the dressing room door.

Bernard (Sumner) is sat at the back of the dressing room with his feet up on the table and he was saying, 'I hate violence, it's just so temporary.' Meanwhile, Hooky is completely cut from different cloth, he has got two empty bottles, he's going, 'Come on! If there's enough of us here we can take 'em!' Hooky's concerned because two of the roadies were out there and they're fighting to save the equipment. Hooky grabs me and shoves two empty beer bottles in my hand, drags me out on to the stage to be confronted with this row of people all just throwing empty pint pots and empty bottles. Hooky meanwhile has now got Tony Wilson hanging on to him by his waist. Hooky's just dragging Tony round this stage shouting, 'Get back in! Get back in!'

It's just happenstance, for want of a better word. It would be fantastic to say, oh, there was a magic that night (June 4, 1976). I think you create your own magic. Yes, it's strange that I met Tony Wilson as a long-haired little gimp that night and later being on Tony's record label. I can't account for it, but I'm not about to romanticise it either.

Wayne Barrett, lead singer of Slaughter and the Dogs, now lives in France. Guitarist Mick Rossi lives in Los Angeles. They come together when required and still perform as Slaughter and the Dogs at punk festivals.

MICK ROSSI: We rehearse in France. Wayne and I sit down and work on our show and what songs we're going to do. As soon as we strike up a chord or whatever there's this little wry smile, yeah ... we've never lost that. There's always that tingle, you know? I remember we did one show in Blackpool at the Winter Gardens. I think it was the third song called 'Boston Babies', which was on *Live at the Roxy,* and just hearing the entire crowd sing the lyrics, you kind of turn round and you go, great, isn't it? It's that little kid in you.

WAYNE BARRETT: I did a couple of mistakes, lyric-wise, and there was these three guys at the Blackpool one and they were singing away. When I made a couple of mistakes on the lyrics they were going (*tutting*) like that and they're correcting me. I had to be really cautious of what I was singing after that, 'cos these three guys were censoring me. The three guys who were doing that, they were like nineteen or twenty.

'No agendas and a lot of fun': Slaughter and the Dogs on stage at the 'Holidays in the Sun' punk festival, Morecambe, Lancashire, July 2000

At the time of writing, Slaughter and The Dogs were planning to celebrate their own silver anniversary at a punk festival in Lancashire.

MICK ROSSI: The Damned, they're going to be doing it. But it's not just like it's the bands that were way back in the early Seventies. It's bands that were in the Eighties, right up to the Nineties, because there still is a healthy movement out there.

WAYNE BARRETT: It all comes back, like the flashback what normal people have. Our flashback, it lasts an hour, where we're banging all the songs out. It's the rehearsal and it's, you remember that? And you start talking. The vibes are still there, which is why I like working with Mr Rossi ...

MICK ROSSI: Thank you, Mr Barrett.

WAYNE BARRETT: The confidence is total. I can turn away when I'm rehearsing and I know what Mike is doing and what he is going to be doing. He knows the same thing and it's like, we don't see each other for, let's say a year, but after around half an hour rehearsing, all that year disappears ... It's amazing how young punks today and the older ones, it's all mixed up. Really mixed up. I mean, they get on really, really well.

MICK ROSSI: It's like a big family, really. So, it's a healthy vibe, no agendas, a lot of fun, no big shakes. Just fun and get out there and have a rocking good time.

Eddie Garrity, otherwise known as Ed Banger, is still playing music and has a new band called Leon.

EDDIE GARRITY: It does seem a long time ago now. The energy is still there, you know, when I play the songs and everything, still do a bit, go out and do the odd gig now and again. At the time I never would have expected it to have lasted to this day where there's still punk bands about. We all thought it would have been over within the first year or something. People were saying punk was dead but I don't think it ever will be, it'll just go on and on.

Audience member Vanessa Corley now runs a vintage clothing shop. Gary Ainsley is a hairdresser; Lorraine Joyce works at Manchester Airport. Ian Moss was also there.

IAN MOSS: The immediate aftermath of the Sex Pistols was that there were bands that were worth making an effort to go and see. I found people who understood the way that I felt. I put a band together and had a thoroughly good time with that as well. The Hamsters was the first band that I had. I had loads of bands, the Bears from Belle Vue Zoo, Mo Mo and the Dodos and numerous others.

When I went to see the Sex Pistols I was training to be a designer in leather goods, and now I'm a shopkeeper. Not very happy.

IAIN GREY: I'm actually in a band now, professionally. A cabaret band called The Steve Ferrigno Band. I play all round Britain.

Malcolm McLaren steered a course through the last quarter of the Twentieth Century that included such ports of call as Sid Vicious, The Great Rock 'n' Roll Swindle, *Ronnie Biggs, Bow Wow Wow, 'Buffalo Gals', scratching, skipping, opera/dance, waltz/dance, films and running for Mayor of London. He is currently writing his memoirs in New York. Pamela Rooke – aka Jordan – is still doing her own thing.*

JORDAN: This is a bit off the wall, really, but I'm a veterinary nurse and I breed Burmese cats and show them. I have some Grand Champion and Champion pussy cats and I love my work. I've been very lucky; always wanted to work with Vivienne and Malcolm, I did. I wanted to work with Adam and the Ants and I did. I subsequently wanted to be a veterinary nurse and I did so. I've basically been asked to do each one, I haven't really had to do much for it, just been kind of lucky, I think. It's a funny thing, because Burmese cats are the punks of the feline world, no doubt about it. They're really very extrovert and they're very youthful – they stay young. I've got a seventeen-year-old who goes bananas, he's barmy. If they could pogo they would. I have always been very anti-nostalgia. Not to say doing documentaries about things is bad – that's great. But I don't like people who constantly live in the past or try to recreate it, because I think it's frankly impossible. I don't think you can recreate it unless you're young. I think it's a young person's thing.

After working in American television, things have come full circle for Chris Pye, the producer of the Pistols' appearance on So It Goes.

CHRIS PYE: Twenty-five years later, I'm now back at Granada, where I'm the Commercial Director, so I'm a businessman. Making programmes is an exciting thing to do, it's a lot of fun. Being a business person, it's a different

Jordan, now a veterinary nurse: 'Burmese cats are the punks of the feline world.' (Photo: Ian Cartwright)

kind of fun. I think that making programmes like *So It Goes* and a few other shows I've made over the years makes you remember what fun it is to be a programme maker. You kind of miss it. Granada business meetings are not held on punk rock lines. I think the legacy of punk is that you can do something that's completely outrageous and raw without really much musical content.

Peter Walker, the Director of So It Goes, *is now semi-retired and lives in Birmingham.*

PETER WALKER: I'm afraid punk, for me, never was an item, never became something I had a collection of at home. Looking back over the last twenty-five years and the things I've personally been involved with, there are three groups who immediately come to mind as being something that changed the way we look at music. I did the sound on *The Doors*, which was a programme that Granada made many, many years ago. I directed the Sex Pistols, which was like a shot in the arm and completely made us re-think. And I did a Wembley OB (outside broadcast) with Talking Heads for the *South Bank Show*. Those three groups immediately come to my mind – they made a hell of a lot of difference. It always amazed me ... later on, when I was working in London, I wandered into the Virgin Megastore on Oxford Street. I was looking up at the monitors where they had videos playing and that was my group (Sex Pistols) on the screen. I couldn't work out why. I thought this was really, really weird. Why are they playing my stuff? I felt I'd done more important things than that, more interesting things than that. Why have they got 'Anarchy in the UK' on? It's only because, from our perspective now, you can look back and say, well, yes, they were something special.

Will Birch, former drummer with the Kursaal Flyers and flag-bearer of all things pub rock, is now an author. On pub rock.

WILL BIRCH: Those groups must have been influenced by Dr Feelgood and Eddie and the Hot Rods. Eddie and the Hot Rods particularly, because they were a bit younger. Course, they all denied it. But now, twenty-five years on, some of them are coming round

The Free Trade Hall and the Lesser Free Trade Hall are currently empty and disused.

PHIL GRIFFIN (writer on architecture): People have been screaming and shouting about it for a number of years now. I can't for the life of me understand why it should have been standing for as many years as it has, with absolutely nothing going on in it. It seems to me a terrible waste of space and it does feel rather as if someone intentionally left the top windows open to allow the pigeons in. It has that feel to it of rather pressurised dereliction. It is important to remember that that street that it sits on, Peter Street, was kind of the Oxford Street, the Soho, the West End of its day. The Gaiety Theatre was on the corner and there were three other theatres alongside it. It's now got a lot of bars on it, but it's worth remembering that the Free Trade Hall has had a position within that entertainment spine. I'd quite like to see it stay and have some sort of public, civic function.

In 1976, Paul Morley was a fanzine scribbler from Stockport. After a run on the New Musical Express *and*

involvement with ZTT records (home of Frankie Goes To Hollywood) as a kind of hype ringmaster, he's now an author. His book Nothing *published in 2000, dealt with the suicide of his father and that of Joy Division's Ian Curtis.*

PAUL MORLEY: The thing about seeing the Pistols at the Lesser Free Trade Hall in 1976 is that it's a curse. I know people of my age that weren't touched by punk – I can spot them a mile off. They're like forty-four-year-olds were in the Seventies and the Sixties and the Fifties. Whereas someone touched by punk at forty-four still kind of has a different approach to life. One thing you could have said to any of us at that gig in '76 was that there was no way on earth that twenty-five years later we would be nostalgic about it. We would have just hated you for suggesting it. But eventually you get to that sort of pipe-smoking, brandy age when you realise it's important to point out how important it was and you're not necessarily being nostalgic.

1976 somehow feels closer now than it did in the Eighties. I think in the Eighties we were racing off, trying to sort of live up to our dreams and do things in a way we'd promised ourselves we would after seeing the Pistols. So it seemed a hundred years ago in the Eighties and now somehow it seems closer and easier to remember. You suddenly say, yeah, I was proud to be there, I was glad I was there.

I've got a funny, dreadful feeling that when we do the fiftieth anniversary – as I suddenly realise we will be – it'll be, oh, it was just like the other day. There was a Manchester City football match in the Sixties, they got their lowest ever attendance when they played someone like Swindon – they got something like 6,000 at Maine Road. Three or four years later they won the Football

League and 72,000 people claimed they were at that Swindon match. I've always had the same thing with the Lesser Free Trade show. But now it seems absurd; how come there were only forty people there? It just seems daft because it was in the *NME*, the Sex Pistols were happening. I guess those people that are embarrassed about the fact that their mums and dads wouldn't let them go and they were too scared of this strange thing that had come up from London, they're now trying to pretend that in fact they were there.

But, I swear I was there. For a long time you would say, 'If you don't believe me, fuck off.' Whereas now, I'm going to stand up and be counted.

Peter Oldham, whose photos provided the inspiration for the book twenty years ago, is now a professional photographer in south Manchester.

Cast of Characters

GARY AINSLEY – AUDIENCE MEMBER.

WAYNE BARRETT – LEAD SINGER OF SLAUGHTER AND THE DOGS.

WILL BIRCH – FORMER DRUMMER WITH THE KURSAAL FLYERS. AUTHOR OF *'NO SLEEP TILL CANVEY ISLAND – THE GREAT PUB ROCK REVOLUTION.'*

VANESSA CORLEY – AUDIENCE MEMBER.

HOWARD DEVOTO – LEAD SINGER OF THE BUZZCOCKS AND LATER OF MAGAZINE.

EDDIE GARRITY – ROADIE AND FUTURE LEAD SINGER OF ED BANGER AND THE NOSEBLEEDS.

IAIN GREY – AUDIENCE MEMBER.

PHIL GRIFFIN – ARCHITECTURAL WRITER.

ALAN HEMPSALL – AUDIENCE MEMBER AND LEAD SINGER OF CRISPY AMBULANCE.

PETER HOOK – BASS PLAYER WITH JOY DIVISION/NEW ORDER/MONACO.

JORDAN – PUNK MUSE – *PUNK ROCK MADE HUMAN* – MAIN FOCUS OF THE SEX PISTOLS' ENTOURAGE .

LORRAINE JOYCE – AUDIENCE MEMBER.

GLEN MATLOCK – BASS PLAYER WITH THE SEX PISTOLS.

MALCOLM MCLAREN – MANAGER OF THE SEX PISTOLS.

IAN MOSS – AUDIENCE MEMBER.

PAUL MORLEY – AUDIENCE MEMBER AND FUTURE *NEW MUSICAL EXPRESS* JOURNALIST.

CHRIS PYE – PRODUCER OF *SO IT GOES* TV SHOW.

MICK ROSSI – GUITAR PLAYER WITH SLAUGHTER AND THE DOGS.

PETER OLDHAM – AUDIENCE MEMBER AND PHOTOGRAPHER.

PETE SHELLEY – GUITAR PLAYER AND LATER LEAD VOCALIST WITH THE BUZZCOCKS.

MARK E. SMITH – LEAD SINGER OF THE FALL.

PETER WALKER – DIRECTOR OF *SO IT GOES* TV SHOW.

TONY WILSON – TV PRESENTER AND FORMER HEAD OF FACTORY RECORDS.

Acknowledgements

Photographs by Ian Cartwright, Rachel Joseph and Peter Oldham. Live footage grabs by Granada Television Graphics (3sixtymedia), Paul Senior and Liz Platt. Thanks to Gary Ainsley, Wayne Barrett, Will Birch, Vanessa Corley, Howard Devoto, Eddie Garrity, Iain Grey, Phil Griffin, Alan Hempsall, Peter Hook, Jordan, Lorraine Joyce, Glen Matlock, Ian Moss, Paul Morley, NWA, Peter Oldham, Chris Pye, Mick Rossi, Pete Shelley, Mark E. Smith, Peter Walker and Tony Wilson. This book is based on interviews and research for the Granada Television documentary *I Swear I Was There*, which was commissioned by Eamonn O'Neal. Good call Eamonn! Thanks to Susanna Wadeson from Granada Books and Peter Walsh from Milo Books for creating 'write me a book' chaos – and to Don Jones from Granada for introducing me to it. Lucy Atkinson and Richard Makinson worked double-time on the programme and did many of the interviews reprinted here. Many gems are down to them. Granada cameramen – especially Paul Watts – recorded the interviews in sound and vision. Julian Coleman edited them for television. Computer guy Paul Vincent took the KAK.WORM virus that was eating the book chapter by chapter out of my computer. Thanks also to Toni Davies for transcribing more tapes than anyone should reasonably be asked to. And to K.M Macfarlane for helping me with computer stuff that remains beyond my understanding.